José Walmir

COPYRIGTH 2017, JOSÉ WALMIR M. DA SILVA

Creativity, Work and Rock & Roll in the Age of Knowledge

All rights reserved and are exclusive property of the writer, and are protected by brazilian federal law 9.610/1998.

It's forbidden the copy or non-autorized reproduction of this work, as a whole or in parts. International eletronic registration 3122339202.

Cover: José Walmir/ Sandra Lira
Edition: José Walmir
Revision: Sandra Lira, Pedro Câmara.

Walmir, José, 1974 -

Original title: Criatividade, Trabalho e Rock'N Roll na Era do Conhecimento
Title: Creativity, Work and Rock & Roll in the Age of Knowledge.

Manaus, Amazonas 2017 1ª edition

1. Education. 2. Economy. 3. Administration. 4. Amazon. 5. Modern Society. 6. Technology. 7. History.

ISBN: 978-17-944-2219-3

jowall2@yahoo.com.br

CONTENTS

1. **Introduction**   09

2. **Human Knowledge**
    1. Knowledge Society.. 18
    2. A History about Knowledge................................ 23
    3. Investing in Knowledge and in Oneself............... 30
    4. The Society of Math's Knowledge........................ 34
    5. Integral Knowledge and its new Scribes.............. 39

3. **Education and Learning**
    1. Brazil, Education, and Everything Else Late....... 48
    2. College Degree, at any cost 53
    3. Failed Education, Bad Productivity..................... 56
    4. The Duty of Raise and Nourish Knowledge......... 59
    5. Rebuilding a Country By Education.................... 63

4. **Jobs and Careers**
    1. The Difficult Art of Valuing Talents.................. 70
    2. The Bad Heritage from the Military Corporation 73
    3. Management, Human Capital and Survival in a Corporation.. 78
    4. Omniscient General-Managers ISO 9999............ 83
    5. Companies Grow Up or Say Goodbye................ 88
    6. Why Work, and to Whom? 93
    7. High Mobility on Jobs: Do they work?............... 97
    8. Work and Grow as a Team, Always.................... 103
    9. Why Companies Need Me?................................ 107
    10. Working in the Age of Knowledge..................... 112
    11. Connecting Much More Than People................. 126
    12. To Work Well, To Live Even Better.................... 148

5. **The Being , the World and the Nothingness**

1. Faith Alone Does not Move Mountains............ 127
2. Failing is easier than trying to succeed............... 131
3. The Art of Merciless Copying n' Pasting............. 136
4. It is difficult to rebuild... 139
5. It is Important Not to be Institutionalized...........144
6. Our Greatest Heritage is the Cultural One......... 148
7. The World of Limitless Information.................... 152
8. Turning Information Into Knowledge................. 156
9. Working and Making the Impossible.................. 160
10. People Will Always Be the Assets....................... 165
11. At Last, Peace... 170

6. **We, in the Amazon Rainforest**

1. Working for the Forest in a World Without Employment... 175
2. Amazon and the Society of Chemical Knowledge... 178
3. The Hub of Worldwide Knowledge.................. 181
4. Microphysics of Knowing.............................. 183

To my mother, to my brothers, to my wife and to my daughters,
who have always inspired me.

In all cultures, social practices are routinely altered in the light of ongoing discoveries which feed into them. But only in the era of modernity is the revision of convention radicalised to apply (in principle) to all aspects of human life, including technological intervention into the material world.

Anthony Giddens

I-Introduction

Listening to the song *"Mother's Little Helper"* by the Rolling Stones, written way back in the 1960's, I do realize how things changed along the years, especially regarding childhood and youth, the most important phases of one's life, the phases that will define who we can be as adults. Besides, we can clearly perceive deep changes that happened in the business market, in the way we see each other, in the way we relate with each other, in medicine, in music, and on the intense addiction in the new technologies, who eases and conditions our daily tasks.

While the music goes on, I keep thinking about the long process of building the country we now know as Brazil, where the laws, the efficient education, the equality in opportunities and actual patriotism were never priorities nor requirements for the raising of a strong, developed, fair and equal nation. Yet, the economical-political elite never had the wits to figure that economic development is the direct result of conjoint, planned actions, where the educational process and the generation of knowledge are central, determining facts, among other variables. The technologic delay left as a legacy generations of citizens of an astonishingly unequal country, failing to value merit and where miserable slums can be found alongside modern buildings, who limit the comfort zone of this small parcel of the population (who tries to pretend that those slums are nothing but a make believe in a Far, Far Away Land) in what became known as *Belindia* – Belgium for some, India for the others.

Knowledge is a process of long-term building, whose main goal is to offer the technical and theoretical foundations to achieve better material conditions, that later will serve as a support to achieve more comfort, security and a positive perspective about the future. It will be operated by generations of individuals, in an endless dialectical process, and it will gather with other's knowledge and shall be revisited under new habits and new researches, making it possible to find a reasonable comprehension of the main conditions acting upon each generation and providing the foundation to whatever will be created or enhanced by the next ones.

Considering the conditions inherited from the country's deficient past, the current generations of Brazilians is formed by professionals issued from a late, defected educational system that lasted for decades, and who opted to fiercely finance their own careers or tried to study abroad as a result of said deficiency. There are also professionals who grew along the changes introduced over the last years and who lack the confidence to believe in the importance of knowledge as an asset to the model of production and organization of the modern society.

The confluence of these professionals under the same work system has shown an array of situations: from flaws in communication to a limited creative capacity, or even the isolation of the talented in an island surrounded by a sea of incertitude. In this scenario, knowledge can be both a fundamental work tool and a minor detail, a support to the traditional systems inherited from an illiterate, misshaped society. Yet, the new methods of business organization, human relations and manufacturing have made the labor routine less brutal and stressful, depending on the workers degree of education, position held in the corporation's hierarchy and specially, how well this worker can handle the new technologies.

It is common sense that the difficulties in the development of educational systems and the lack of a wide variety of efficient knowledge stagnate the optimization and technical improvement of the three generations of workers acting on today's business market. This does not allow that said workers work themselves up to a strategic position in the nation's social groups, which would help the solution or at least the mitigation of many problems related to the communities, the enterprises or the government in Brazil, as well as cultivating the national science and the feeling of citizenship.

The dominant conception of the current scientific zeitgeist, which serves as base to the knowledge appropriation by worldwide, private economic groups, helped shaping the way the intellectual capital is used and valued, and its exploitation by the corporations. Considering that knowledge is the main fountain of wealth generation in the modern age, the sheer possession of natural resources no longer means the certainty of success or condition to a nation's growth, like back in the Navigation's times or the Industrial Revolution. Owning resources does nothing to a nation's social or economic development if there is not a source of knowledge applied to the main structures and chains of production, making possible the extraction of goods and reverting them to the country's security and comfort, especially if it is a non-renewable natural resource.

The data we have nowadays consider that nowadays the difficulties to find job or to be reinserted in the market effectively are much more difficult, whether by the lack of experience or by the delimitation of minimal requirements necessary for a career or a job.

The work environment has become way more automatized and it's demands way more complex and particular, in a world where the last transformations shaped the way we behave, think and produce, causing a heavy confluence of processes connected by the same work focus and ideas, but with different ways of integration among different workplaces spread over the globe.

It is relevant to consider that Science, applied to the material needs of individuals, has been offering more and more products, services, ideas and efficient solutions, besides offering higher quality of abstract knowledge that sometimes does not fit properly in the traditional knowledge, and often finds trouble trying to coherently (or at least, feasibly) be inserted in one the thousands theories about souls, environment, evolution, personalities, technologies or the eternal life (which some of us, human beings, try to develop no matter how, even if it means to be put in cryogenic sleep waiting a miracle). It's a society that calls itself post-modern, post-industrial, post-presence, *where time and space are apart from practical life*[1], and tends to be even more abstracts as concepts, generating an array of behaviors and actions away from the main context, where life starts being practiced or influenced by the optic fiber's networks or the wi-fi.

The scientific breakthrough has also contributed to the decline of the largest western religion, the Christianism, and left the world even more unstable and not so sure of the idea of be reborn alongside Jesus, since the new belief is to try not to die at all (or at least to live 500 years). In this new, godless world, without prophets to show the ways to follow, people are slowly being *stripped away of a universal history, and without it, they feel free from any absolute truth, being left alone in a world without references and open to every possibilities*[2], including terrorism, hate against thy neighbor, intolerance or simply abstract loneliness, shared only with the computer technologies to hide away some inner emptiness.

In this world of absolute relativity, where kids are born "already knowing it all", even intelligence (like time and space) has become relative, and there is a stapled perception that it is developed according to the kid's aptitudes and skills, in dimensions way beyond refined musical perception or complex mathematical proceedings. Alongside the "over amplified" family, made up by parents, close relatives, and the world wide web, who plays a large role in the education, points of view and traits a kid will develop, being the perception of what's the world far wider than the motherly house, but the actual world.

These traits, observed both in and outside the familiar and corporate environment, indicate that not only the world is changing at a fast pace but *we are moving into one in which the consequences of modernity are becoming more radicalized and universalized than before*[3], as Giddens pointed out. It is a necessity to have another pedagogical model, alternative ways to administrate the subjects and a new method of collaborative learning, where it is possible to bind the best techniques of teaching and individual skills to the process of generating and sharing knowledge, whose focus is unclear in our country and its promotion is not precise.

Considering, still, that the process of education in Brazil and in the Amazon was achieved through precarious conditions of learning, aggravating the lack of perception of the differential nature of modern knowledge and contributing to a significant limitation in the quality and technical capacitation of the professionals, it is possible to perceive that nowadays, the promises and projects made in the past about the country's future were not concluded, and the time and resources lost in this period of time will never return. The old practices of bad public management still active, thanks to the political populism and paternalism, besides the disproportionate costs between the main and intermediate activities and the astonishing corruption in the public system, which impoverish the population and weakens the democracy.

The public educational system in our country, through the strenuous and memorization-based process of admission into the prestige universities, has brought to an extreme the ferocious, excluding competition, while doing nothing to develop in public school students the perception of knowledge as the world more advanced competitive tool. Very few people pursuit an extended, post-graduation investment for their careers. As the public educational system has remained obsolete down to its core, most of the more financially stable families have been spending more and more resources on their child's education, either in costly private institutions or by sending them to study abroad, as to provide them with a higher level of knowledge the small "elite" cannot find in the national education system. In a deeply unequal country, this kind of gap in knowledge and academic production between the upper classes and the more modest ones has become abyssal. Considering the limitation in vacancies for the most important Universities, they end up becoming an exclusive oasis for the children of the same wealthy families, concentrating 50% of the nation's income and excluding from their ranks other talented people who were less adapted to the strict admission exam.

The process of generating knowledge is structured through educational tools built and valued in a given society, shaped after the considerations inherited from the elderly generations to serve some objective practice. Nowadays, most of the knowledge produced applies to the technological intervention in the real world and its productive and organizational grounds. The lack of objectivity and efficiency on the educational system directly implies in the quality of professional and vocational training, limits the work's productivity, stagnates the country's economy, maintains the levels of poverty and constrain the exercise of citizenship in our society. It allows the maintenance of the dishonest, immoral economic advantages of those who profit the most of the country's resources, and who spend this money later on the artificial paradises around the world.

The Amazon, even though is one of the most fascinating regions in the world, has no conditions to grant to its own population any sort of undisputable protection, since the academic knowledge grounds accumulated in the region fall short in relation to the overall of possibilities that often are gazed upon it. There is a latent necessity of building a modern structure that allows the interaction between humans and the green paradise in a clean, conscious, safe and symbiotic form, having as founding principle the generation of knowledge about itself and how it bonds to numerous other global proceedings.

The first great concern about the Amazon was about international pressure over the exploitation of its rivers and internationalization of its biological content, which, for the most part are still alive and more dynamics than initially thought. Another threat is the presence of an everlasting illegal timber industry, usually issued from the southwestern region, causing irreparable damage to the environment, mainly in the southernmost part of the region. Currently, west of the state of Amazonas, it's perceived the destruction of natural biomes in favor of psychotropic monoculture, the loss of spatial sovereignty, threats to the population's safety and theft of resources by drug cartels issued from Colombia and Peru makes it even more difficult to the government's legal structures to reach such remote locations.

The Amazon stands for a gigantic world of possibilities, for better or worse, depending on who can profit from it in the efficient way. Be it by trying to the turn its natural resources in beneficial solutions for everyday issues, be it by using its space as a hideout for criminal practices, be it by illegally exploring its flora and fauna, or be it by simply protecting the forest's biomes as a way to guarantee an ecological future. Only the military or government's presences in the region is no safekeeping of the productive possibilities the forest can proportionate to its inhabitants, and does not poses any support to building up any knowledge, except for the one applied to self-defense or to survival of a few.

In a regional, more concerning, scenario, some questions must be analyzed about the problems of knowing and generating knowledge in the Amazon, which has become not only the last frontier of Brazilian colonization but also a minority shareholder, financial dependent and beggar for governmental interventional policies regarding security, economy, research and utilization of its wide resources. Its ample ecosystem can contribute to the generation of wealth and tends to influence and condition the worldwide process of production in the post-industrial era.

Still, even if we tried by other means, the assurance of sovereignty of our rich region must necessarily go through the construction of a system of generation of structural knowledge about Amazon's biomass. It must be bound to the local necessities of local inhabitants, targeting to guarantee the control of the generated knowledge, making it possible to synthetize with the means already stapled and available to utilization. This situation can only be founded by a system who values people, institutions and process related to the specific purposes and needs of the regional inhabitants.

In a world where Science is the new religion and knowledge became the most important part of most governments and corporation's schedules, no nation have the luxury to deny to its children the right to know, to try to explore, to find out what's yet to be found. As such, it is much more necessary the structuration of modern educational systems, efficient and commited, put as a fundamental support to the equilibrate research of answers to a better life in community, especially in such an exclusive region as Amazon.

To know itself and know to put itself in this wide world, full of dreams and possibilities, is to be able to live and dream altogether, where the development of the useful capacities (that can contribute to turning dreams into reality or vice-versa) are being taught in elementary school or at home, complementing in a constructive and shared manner, and that later can be turned into vices and routines whose objective is to learn how to learn, even in tough, barely comfortable situations.

It seems that only recently it is maturing in our country the notion that other modern societies are centered around knowledge as economical-social value. Even considering that some structural deficits inherited from a recent past made it harder to take position and perform well professionally and limited the level of produced knowledge, it is still possible to be more efficient, productive and creative, no matter from which generation you're issued, by utilizing modern tools and adopting a posture focused on gathering necessary knowledge to the evolution of people and companies. Those who managed to do so will live a longer, safer and well-adjust professional life.

It is certain that knowledge and discipline to acquire it are the dominant factors in careers and professions, and made possible a largest income to families, governments and companies who wish to invest upon it. Following this logic, the greatest legacy we can possibly leave to our children is the cultural legacy, constituted by the bases of fundamental knowledge, upon which they shall built their interpretation and interactions with the world in a healthy, organized manner. By supporting their ideas and answers to the world's problems, or at least their own world's problems, can pave the way to a better, more productive adult life.

Lastly, my dear mother tells me every Saturday: "only Jesus saves". It must be a deep truth, however, in human's relations with their environments and people they share their mundane, average lives, only knowledge frees. We cannot run away from this affirmative for a long, everlasting time, because without knowledge about itself and about its possibilities, we cannot create better conditions to achieve our goals. Tine fades away, ferociously eating up our hopes and energies, until we realize what is important, and the opportunities we've left behind, and when time turns itself against us and we can only turn to some colored pills to make us live painless, like on the lyrics of the beautiful song by the Rolling Stones[4]:

> "'Kids are different today',
> I hear every mother say
> Mother needs something today to calm her down
> And though she's not really ill..."

References to Introduction:

1 Zigmynt Bauman, **Liquid Modernity**, 1999.
2 Neiza Teixeira, **Para Aquém e para Além de Nós,** 2012.
3 Anthony Giddens, **Consequences of Modernity**, 1990
4 Rolling Stones, album **Aftermath,** 1966, Capitol Records.

> I do not feel obliged to believe that the same God who has endowed us with sense, reason, and intellect has intended us to forgo their use.
> Galileo Galilei

II – HUMAN KNOWLEDGE

Knowledge has always been somewhat unsettling along the human trajectory, acquiring a more relevant status since the process of Sedentism took place, evolving into a wider political organization called "State", setting up new forms of coexistence, production, thinking, behaving and relating to other human beings. Some ancient cultures believe that their cultural level, economic status and warfare technology made them racially superior to other races, who needed to be "taught better", according to their standards.

On the Book of Genesis after the claimed creation of the first humans, God advises against eating the forbidden fruit, because if so they did, they would be ruthlessly condemned to death. Such prohibition produced, in said societies, the notion that acquiring knowledge would be a disrespectful activity against God's laws, and therefore the pursuit of science would be but for a few ones, handpicked individuals by god who were blessed with a message that God himself wanted to make public. Along the godly restraints, mankind developed a symbolical system of communication who most people didn't knew about were not used on everyday activities, a system controlled and maneuvered by those who had "disposition" to crack that code, the written code as we know, who acquired new dimensions as the years went by, until the development of programming language.

Knowledge Society

Stairway to Heaven is the title of a song by the famous British group Led Zeppelin, found on its fourth studio album, issued in 1971. The decades of 1960 and 1970 produced the greatest rock n' roll groups of all times, and also made possible the development of the most important technologies utilized on the next decades. Ever since then, people started to realize that effectively society was changing at a fast pace, and its main structures (family, relationships, jobs and works) were walking towards a new model of social and organizational model, alongside new geopolitics and economics, powered up by the development and spread of modern personal computers. They improved the capacity of production, leisure and work, allowed the processing of huge quantities of data and made available the access to information through huge networks of digital interaction –the internet–, contributing in a decisive way to the advancement of financial and economics market, being somewhat a product and active agent of the shift in values idealized by the youth of the explosive rock n' roll radio decades.

In 2006, Capra sustains that the determining factor of the main changes happening in societies' structures begins in *its 'paradigm shift' (*From the Greek paradeigma ("pattern").) - a profound change in the thoughts, perceptions, and values that form a particular vision of reality*[1].When a shared world vision, like the pattern of behaviors and traditional knowledge are revisited under a new values, they begin to determine each individuals comprehension about its own condition, meaning and existential duty.

Any change in the comprehension of the main set of values in a given social structure begins in the wide reformulation of the methods to investigate reality, of the way knowledge is built and how technologies can be upgraded after it, and gradually leaving out the other ways of comprehension and knowledge that no longer fit the new reality accordingly. That happened ever since the Neolithic Revolution, and after that consecutively in Socratic Greece, then the Hellenistic Era, the Christianism's expansion, the European Renaissance, the navigations to the America, the Enlightenment, and in a deepest way, the Modern Industrialism, which became clearer in the post-industrial world where the scientific method of investigation became no only predominant but nearly exclusive.

Peter Drucker was not the first scholar to research about the functioning, traits and area of impact in the knowledge society. However, he was a pioneer and one of the most prolific scientists to ever dedicate part of his studies to the analysis of the causes, consequences and possibilities of this new society in a global scale. In an article published in 1970, he pointed out that one of the most important long-term resources would be the emerging of a mass career's market to the qualified professionals whose field of work is the knowledge[2].

At the time, maybe most of the professionals and enterprises haven't yet noticed, but the economic sector that was about to become more dynamic, employing more people and producing more riches would be the Services Sector, instead of the Industrial, who maintained this post for over 200 years. Therefore, the new economic setup would demand another profile in learning and professionalizing, and company's organization would have to have ever-changing structures in the pursuit of innovation, whereas established the new perception of knowledge as the main source of economic wealth. The professionals who managed to perceive quickly the new terms and anticipated the facts began earlier to put themselves ahead of the best enterprises and business in the next few years, when the intellectual capital became vital to the most dynamic companies.

Currently in any environment, be it home or enterprise, the utilization of computers, tools and I.T. systems organize and coordinate the everyday activities, in a deeply natural synergy, becoming essential to any field of activity in human, modern life. However, in the '70s, many professionals could not realize the changes that were occurring both in careers and in organization, especially regarding the "digital revolution" taking place. As such, they were gradually being excluded from the professional market or losing competitiveness to new brands built under a new operational and organizational point of view. This happened to Xerox, the first company to ever develop a personal computer, which was never put to market, as to quote one of its CEOs, because "the computer will never be as important to society as the copy machine"[3].

Nevertheless, other professionals perceived such changes as not superficial or simple, but so deep that would legate their children a completely different world from theirs. So, they listened to the lyrics of Led Zeppelin's song, when it says *"yes, there are two paths you can go by, but in the long run, there's still time to change the road you're on*". And changing the road, at the time, meant to search further training in-company, learn to work and to think using the newest tools, to develop new skills, to accept ambiguity as something healthy, to try to fit into any new institutional environment in a productive manner alongside professionals issued from different backgrounds and different fields. Changing the road meant to be the sole responsible for your own time management, your own process and progress and your own results, and being always willing to learn again and change again whenever needed. In that decade, Peter Drucker already advised that "the center of gravity of the American work force has been shifting from manual worker (...) to the *Knowledge Worker* with a very high degree of formal schooling"[4] and the ability to interact with tools who worked on a specific computational platform.

The decade of 1970 would produce some of the global companies that have revolutionized all the global economics with the technological creation and innovation. In 1972, Nolan Bushnell founded Atari, Inc in California, focusing on electronic game's production. In 1975, Bill Gates and Paul Allen founded Microsoft. In 1976, along his friend Steve Wozniak, Steve Jobs founded Apple. In 1975 began the commercialization of the first personal computer of the modern age, the Altair 8800, inaugurating Intel's microprocessors, a new, innovative company founded in 1968.

In 1979, the rock n' roll group AC/DC released their sixth album, christened Highway to Hell, the last one with the legendary frontman Bon Scott. The album's name announced exactly what the decade of 1980 became to many companies and workers who became obsolete when the winds of the Information Era began to blow harder, and the need to reinvent the professional career urged. By the end of that decade, many who did not manage to appropriate themselves effectively of the essential, new work tools and social interactions, were violently thrown into second-class jobs or the rising wave of unemployment.

Also in 1979, the English band Pink Floyd released their highest grossing LP, The Wall. The album dealt with questions related to the ultraconservative educational model in the UK and with some mental "misconceptions" that generation carried within after the intense abuse of heavy drugs in earlier years, which resulted in an extremely different point of view than the one their parents inherited. That would make the *youth culture (...) the matrix of the cultural revolution in the wider sense of revolution in values and customs, in ways of spending leisure and in commercial arts*[5.]

The knowledge society was "created" when advanced science began to intervene more in systematic chains of production, enhancing the array of products and solutions to everyday problems, and in a lesser scale due to the new world views of that generation. This intervention reached deeply the social structures, particularly families, through a new posture in familiar relations, new methods of raising and teaching children and a newfound way of "programming" birth and the amount of wanted children, thus "liberating" the sexual practice.

The surge of a society focused on knowledge made possible for science to create tools and ideas more and more focused on financial return such interventions could bring, therefore creating the character of the "specialized professionals", who deeply dedicates themselves to a field of research. One of the fields science took more interest (motivated by the high chances of fortune and possibly fame) was computer's science, especially in mass media communications and interactions with other systems, tools and personal services, resulting in the building and mass access to thousands of products who uses operational basis some sort of computational system. These technological gadgets are also being progressively used in medical diagnosis, helping to find and treat new diseases the human body would usually perishes from, by anticipating them and guaranteeing a longer lifespan and who knows, maybe in the future, eternal youth can be achieved through costly cosmetics and more exclusive, expensive and accurate medical treatment.

The companies born under this operational perspective, who dedicated themselves to create and offer high-tech, costly products and services, quickly became worldwide giants, and for some time dominated the stock market around the globe, rivaling against traditional, huge companies that for decades grasped their market. As a result, after two decades the Information Era companies incorporated most of these traditional enterprises, led by innovative, creative and highly qualified young men. Accordingly to the classification of the BrandZ ranking, elaborated annually by WPP and Millward Brown[6], among the 10 most valuable enterprises in the world, eight worked in technology and information sector: Google, Apple, Microsoft, AT&T, Facebook, Amazon, Verizon and IBM.

In this list, only IBM and AT&T were not built during the decade of 1970, but had to reinvent themselves in a small timespan due to the impositions of the new technological perspectives and legal disposition. By absorbing the more updated ideas of the young innovators, who were less bound to the industrial environment and who believed in a new way the world could be arranged, those companies started to picture this world after the possibilities the new technologies could make available in a near future. Furthermore, the computational technology developed or enhanced in the 70's generated an spectacular raise in the capacity of processing information, *that made possible a greatest integration in business systems, resulting in the discovery of a new integral knowledge*[7]. It became the fundamental part of the management and operational structures of the rising companies, especially among the more "intense" sectors in technology utilization, who progressively showed to be profitable.

In late nations as Brazil, at the same time, the data processing was controlled and centered around a government so pointless that General Geisel himself decided to end the Military Regime, because even he saw what a huge mess it was, with little to zero capacity to process information and without and ideological conditions to let the population do it by themselves. Even worse was that the information and generation of knowledge were controlled by the official censorship, which used archaic methods to select the contents that could be published.

Few Brazilians – except the ones in exile – perceived what was happening in that post-industrial era world, where the new dominant social and economic structures were being built. Among these few, in 1978, the group Legião Urbana questioned in an aggressive tone, trait of a youth unsatisfied with the military savagery: what country was that? Miserably rich, politically excluding, deeply illiterate and deprived of institutions that could allow the construction of solid bases to the promotion of citizenship as much as the lack of an universalist teaching system, based upon a modern pedagogy, committed with the integral formation of the national citizen and integrated with the new conditions to create and process knowledge.

When the decade of 1980 rushed into and information began to circulate more freely around the country, it was finally possible to have an exact and tragic notion of how late and third world we were. Late, impoverished, semiliterate, and everyday farther away from the best democratic practices, from better industrial management, from the real generation of knowledge, from the development in researches and from the industrial and commercial levels to revert this retard inherited from the structures of the past. This crisis inspired a new generation of artists, which reflected in the content of their speeches against the nation's political and socio-economical system, especially regarding misery, corruption, wealth accumulation, the means of communication and the passive posture of the Brazilian people, quiet while facing the everyday problems that most of the population must go through. These representations became eternal in a generations mind, through books, movies and memorable songs like Desordem (Disorder) in 1987, by one of the great gods of Brazilian Rock, the Titãs, which sums up what they thought about the "lost years":

> The convicts flee the prison, pics on the TV
> One more hooligan's fight ends up in confusion
> The crowd pissed off, burn the cop's car
> The convicts go insane, what a crazy nation!
> Is it not an attempt of suicide to go the other way?
>
> Os presos fogem do presídio, imagens na televisão.
> Mais uma briga de torcidas, acaba tudo em confusão.
> A multidão enfurecida, queimou os carros da polícia.
> Os presos fogem do controle, mas que loucura esta nação!
> Não é tentar o suicídio querer andar na contramão?

A History About Knowledge

For a long time, a fundamental question imposed itself firmly over the basis of knowledge, under different guises and pretexts, in given conditions and diverse environments: What is our true origin, and where are we going, considering that we are progressively enhancing our mental capacities and increasing the level of understanding about the conditions that produce and sustain the biological and psychic life? This question has become deeply relevant in certain situations, because we are probably never going to be able to accept that, deep down, we are not the wonderful creatures that God itself had the pleasure to create, raise and care after his image and godhood. Nonetheless, to many of our own species, the simple fact that such questions became the start of countless, even bigger issues and forced the development of a new logical system of structural learning was already worthy of an entire, meaningful life, rich in content and belief that in any moment of our intellectual search, we started believing faithfully in our ancestry as the children of the god's in a superior realm.

On the other hand, through a long process of questioning intensified on the Classic Antiquity, the search for knowing who we are became more and more complex, mainly because the human being cannot accept peacefully the end of life as something natural and essential to the working of the Universe, moreover by the honesty of a few men, who in accept the fact that we will never know who we are. This doubt led the human species in a constructive, productive race for some kind of knowledge that could unveil its identity, calm its simple minds an try to answer the true meaning of our existence in this wide, unknown universe, while we wait the unavoidable call of the death, which could lead us to our own true essence.

The long search for comprehension of ourselves (or at least the meaning we give to this comprehension) begins somewhere around a moment of deep change in material life's conditions, when the threes vanished from the landscape and were replaced by large grassland plains, where the eldest ancestors of the human were completely unprotected from the great emptiness. As such, facing the possibility of extinction and without knowing God had created them, this "apes" had to craft some form of essential knowledge, different from the set of genetic skills they inherited from their ancestors and were common among rivalling animals, in order to thrive in this less than safe environment.

It is not possible to argue precisely, but it is very likely that the beginning of the search for a more accurate, more "true" type of knowledge may have started as a necessity to the survival of the human species itself against a gigantic, unexplained world, especially face to our species lack of fitness in comparison with other great mammals. After guaranteeing the survival and imposing themselves as the ruling biological form on the planet, our ancestors showed a passionate interest in widening the conscious search for the mechanics and correlations that conditions life on Earth, inside an even bigger shared environment. Later, it inevitably escalated into the search to discover how an organism can sustain its own life, aware of its own consciousness, and manipulating it with the purpose of relieving us of the of any uncertainty regarding existence and even the great trauma of biological death. Therefore, humankind advanced, accepting the knowledge of the past societies in a non-absolute manner, accepting its flaws and its limitations as fundamental to its own expansion from a given baseline inherited knowledge and search to widen its sources, means, applications and purposes as a way to enrich the accumulated knowledge from the past. In the end, the goal is to optimize the organization of the social group, its mechanisms of material production and its instruments of power, control, heal and entertainment.

The accumulation of knowledge about nature (and about men inserted in its environment) became essential to the social organization and constitute major asset to secure people's survival in larger settlements, determining and coordinating the structures of crops, the understanding the seasons, the counting the supply of food, the paying of tributes, the security of the settlement, the exploration natural resources, structuring knowledge and the organizational complex between the state, the army and the spirituality.

As the knowledge expanded and amplified human intervention over nature, gradually it attained a god-like status, as if God offered it to men himself, consolidating it as the main source of power to those who held its control as it was the only way to achieve a universal, higher level of wisdom. As a result, the central power binds knowledge and constantly tries do influence it. The conjoint society of the central, political – real – power and the divine – clerical – power enhanced the organization of states submissive to the image of a divine king counseled by priests and beloved by its vassals as the representation of God on Earth, a king who deserved absolute obedience and reverence, undoubtable in its actions.

The union between State and church intensified to the point they became nearly the same structure, showing great efficacy on its administration and securing enough social stability to justify the egocentric stravaganza of a monarchic power with divine aspirations. The society began to be coordinated by an efficient, cultured bureaucracy, solidified by an institution considered the only interpret between God and humankind. It started to determine what life is and what death should be, to theorize, write, ritualize and teach that the unexplainable facts in life are, in fact, irrefutable manifestations of God's will, guiding humankind through time to the place He wants it to achieve someday.

Unlike the old structures of polytheist religions, which in spite of having many different deities had a ruling liege god, the process of explaining Life's phenomena after the divine wisdom under the optics of one all-mighty God made possible the construction of a much more organized ecclesiastic structure, with a missionary vocation, trying to universalize through the other's conversion. The Catholic Church, built under Paul, became much more radical in its mission after the self-proclaimed Christian imperator Constantine the Great, who made tolerable the practice of the Christian faith all over the Roman Empire and influencing on the interpretation of God's words after his own vision. He sought to place himself above the State, the customs and human reason, resulting in a new political and social organization and in a new form of attaining knowledge, conditioned by the "Jewish Bible" and disregarding every non-spiritual experience.

In this period, in the western European world and proximities, the Catholic Church organized and consolidated itself as the main political, administrative ant theological structure. Since the fall of the Roman Empire and thanks to the structures they inherited from the old society, the Church began to monopolize, edit, censor and limit the access, production and circulation of knowledge, holy or secular, in any sphere that could be attributed to a divine miracle.

The intellectual structure raised by the christening of western society forged new ways of thinking, acting, and living, and corroborate to the fact that on the Middle Age, the intellectuals were mostly catholic, with a theoretical basis on few more ancient Christian theologians, the Bible, Aristotle and Plato. Only after the separation between the State and the Church, the production and divulgation of researches over another subjects unrelated to the catholic faith was made possible.

For the most part of that period, the main intention and function of educational systems and generation of knowledge was to legitimize the cultural inheritance already practiced. Furthermore, it sustained with theoretical basis the policies of governments and the ecclesiastics' actions, just as the formality of laws being almost one with religious tradition *where the typical ruler paid the priests, philosophers and poets hoping they would legitimize his power and keep social order*[8].

Many intellectuals of the Christian age built their works to the eternity after the catholic point of view over the event: from the facts of life to the mysteries of death. St. Thomas Aquinas, St. Isidore of Seville, St. Bernard of Clairvaux, and Dante Alighieri himself, who produced his monstrous work, the Divine Comedy, after the last part of the Bible according to the new "operational structure" the church created to administrate the post-mortem of its followers who could afford indulgences to mitigate their sufferings. As stated by Jacques Le Goff in his classical "Medieval Calling", asserts that the Comedy have the status of a third Testament, like an apocryphal Gospel[9]. The Comedy made possible the production of many other works about the point of view of men of late medieval period, challenging the morals and values established in that society. After the invention of the press, countless other works, in literature and science, started to spread out of the Church's control. The Middle Age ends with a magnificent wave of reformulation and reinterpretation of the age's knowledge, alongside many movements born against the structures in politics, religion and especially cultural. The Reformation, the Renaissance, the formation of national stats, the exploration of America, the European Mercantilism; A largely different world presented itself in three hundred years. These changes propelled a new set of material knowledge, whose main trait was the detachment of the biblical, theological lore as a reliable source of information. Ever since, a spectacular advance in technology and perception took place, and the necessity to create a structural system of producing knowledge unbound from traditional sources urged. The publication of pioneer workpieces proposed a method of investigation method who could explain the facts and nature's phenomena: the Scientific Method. It culminated in a boom of works, experiments, and advanced ideas to improve the method, the purpose and conditions to investigate phenomena:

> The wave of discoveries, made on many scientific fronts, were the Works of hundreds of hobby scientists, stargazers, medical men and clergy with an hour to spare. Many were all-rounders who were intent on solving a cluster of intellectual riddles.[10]

After the publication of important works by Descartes, Galileo, John Locke and Newton, a new system of thinking and investigating began to build up, detaching even more the Christian considerations and focusing on the search of coherent explanations and methods to comprehend the universe's laws and general conditions that could influence life, culminating in the European Enlightenment. This movement legated to the world great works that became references in their fields for a long period, like Locke's "Two Treatises of Government", Rousseau's "The Social Contact", Kant's "Critique of Pure Reason", among others.

The reformulation of the educational process, the change in perception about life in society, the scientific rational research and the gradual application of systematic knowledge to ancient process of manufacture created the necessity of the organizations and institutions to search for "different" minds, who could work in the development of new inventions or improvement of methods, for the continual refinement of research techniques, public administration or the knowledge generation itself.

The Industrial Revolution was more than just a machinery revolution aimed at the production of material goods: it changed the basis of all structures fundamental to the working of society, even the perception of God, untouched for thousands of years.

The first industrials were either engineers or financially associated to them, and used their inventions in their own workplaces or shops to ameliorate products manufactured by hand or in small factories, leading to the process of industrial-scale production that would influence humanity's radical changes over the next few centuries. The new machinery not only enhanced capacities and muscle-based power, but also the "Industrial civilization gave technology sensory organs, creating machines that could hear, see, and touch with greater accuracy and precision than human beings"[11].

Along the development of the Industrial Revolution, and since the moment this chain of production confirmed to have a large advantage over the traditional methods and could lead to a fairer society by the production of larger amounts of wealth, a new philosophical movement was born, defined by the belief in humanity's supposed objective rationality: the Positivism. Embodying the methodologic rigor of the scientific investigation and the unshaken confidence in the intellectual production reached through human race, the Positivism sought the analysis of the changes happening in Europe, and spread among all the fields of human intellectual production, especially in Humanities, were it preached that knowledge, systemic and structural, could free all humankind from the shackles the Nature imposed to all species.

The consolidation of this rational, objective model of thinking proportionated the development of countless theories and relevant works that would change the human vision about themselves and natural facts once again. Works like Darwin's "On the Origin of Species", Weber's "The Protestant Ethic and the Spirit of Capitalism", Marx's "Capital: Critique of Political Economy" and Einstein's theory on General Relativity, Mendeleev's work on the classification of the chemical elements, etc. changed hugely the way human beings perceive and act upon the world. Increasingly, humans *"came to believe they could increase their capabilities by investing in scientific research"*[12] and it could lead us to a better understanding of life's phenomena and universal laws without the figure of a Central God.

Ever since, the structuration of the thinking systems became more sophisticated, and its production became priority to many countries, enterprises and families, who started to see in knowledge a substantial assurance of better life's condition and the building of a more democratic, equal society. The perception that knowledge also frees is soothing and pleasing, and made possible the constitution of more advanced products, services and process, the so-called technologies, which nowadays are found in every field of human life, from the cooking of food to the perception of pleasure.

Still, the structured knowledge made possible the construction of countless tools, theories, specific rules and investigation devices, essential to people's everyday life, from enhancing life to avoiding death. Besides, it serves as technological basis to its own system of industrial production, in what Toffler defined as a technological womb, a system that is *"inventing machines designed to give birth to new machines in infinite progression"*[13].

This world vision grew in the society the conviction that safe and comfortable life maintenance is directly linked to the level of graduation and knowledge one can apply somewhere for economic ends. In this long process, the scientific knowledge became central, by the capacity it developed of reproducing in a secure, efficient manner, different from the older investigation devices. Besides, this kind of knowledge started to be the more dynamic and efficient form of structuring the modern industrial system of production, that start to use uses these "theories in order to acquire new powers, and in particular to develop new technologies"[14] who will be incorporated to the new globalized system. As such, the conceptual basis and the available structure of any system of knowledge is fundamental to motivate people willing to comprehend and widen it, raising the level of knowledge and, alongside it, the possibility of a more equal, wealthy and dynamic world; healthier, more stable and less influenced by the fear of the limitations brought by death and illness.

In the Classical Antiquity, the necessity of comprehending what was allegedly the divine will and how it could influence existence lead man to the acquisition of fundamental knowledge and the search for reasonable – or convenient – explanations about the functioning of life and its consequences. In the modern world, the necessity of being God (or being at least close to Him), is leading people to seek knowledge to the last barriers of rationality and objectivity of humankind's existence, realizing that they can no longer submit to an almighty God who can control or manipulate people and nature at His will without remorse, guilt or fear, because gods are fearless and remorseless in their actions.

Investing in Knowledge and in Oneself

In the last years, publishing market flooded in countless works about the values and attitudes that guides the professional success, the productivity and the way high-performance professionals, called "gifted", contribute or influence in the construction of efficient work methods, technical formation and management of winning teams. These talented professionals came to be perceived as the more competitive differential an enterprise have to aggregate value to its products, brands and global commercial services, in a new socioeconomic environment convention calls society of knowledge. The last fifty years were of extreme technologic advance, especially in the central countries of the developed world. Still in the decade of 1960, modern societies started to perceive more strongly the unbalance in wealth distribution around the globe. After, one of the reasons verified was the brutal gap in the educational systems between the richer and the poorer countries, especially those legated to the permanent status of "third world". In this period, knowledge became one of the more important variables, and focused people alongside the more dynamic companies started to invest on its production, through academic formation, research and expansion, or the building of R&D – research and development – departments, constituted by directly employees from those enterprises or by private groups of scientists financed by the government or particular groups interest in their researches.

This mentality of investing in R&D, initially based on the constant need companies have to compete for a better market position was gradually migrating to the Research and Extension departments at prestige Universities, who prioritized works that could turn to profit. The next step was to prioritize among the scholars, teachers and students, which could contribute the most to achieve this profit. It created a large raise in demand of courses aimed at it, at the expense of the courses who could not fit properly to the governmental or industrial needs. The technological R&D "became central to the economic growth, and for this reason, the already enormous advantage of the 'developed market economies' over the rest was reinforced"[15]. The less developed economies started even to depend on the technologies produced by the former, when the years of research started paying with a high financial return.

This situation, powered by the fact that the new technologies needed less and less people to operate them, raised the levels of unemployment and underemployment and sought to give the best paying jobs to people who worked in the development or effective operation of the new technologies introduced in this productive system. In return, the demand for technical courses immensely rose, especially in the advanced medical areas, engineering and reengineering, courses related to computational process like mechatronics, game engineering, nano and biotechnology, besides researches in the functioning of the brain, aerospace technology and cybernetics.

In the central countries, the educational question was often a relevant issue for the State, who saw in that process a safe way to remain significantly strong, wealthy and sovereign, and where a significant part of the public and private investment turned to researches directed to the improvement of the means of production, innovation, security, health and new adjoined technologies. However, in later and poorest countries like Brazil, the education offered (especially in the public sector) was historically limited and deficient, and when the State tried to expand the absolute number of students, the academic quality fell to even lower levels. Today, the educational system constitutes one of the most negative variables of the public investment in peripheral, late countries, like ours.

This negativity of the public education, along the high economical value that formal education achieved, made the families of the whole country and the Amazonas state – particularly Manaus – to dispend higher sums of financial resources on their children's education, hoping that they could offer the possibility to build a solid and stable professional career in valued or to-be-valued areas. More and more families are proposing themselves this objective, overflowing the classes of highly competitive schools that claim to have the best results in the best universities' selective process, joining the families that long ago realized this was *the* best way of winning them a better income, but, above all, a higher social stats[16] in a deeply unequal country.

Long ago, a vision still shared among lots of families in Brazil is that educational costs are overwhelming expenses, or that they should be an unconditional obligation of the government. However, considering the high value of knowledge, these costs are not expenses; they are essentially investments in human and intellectual capital, one of the most advanced factors of competitiveness nowadays, so relevant that the most prepared institutions and people charge high values to offer it. The solid reputation such institution have can make possible for its graduated students and disciples to have a higher general recognition for those who seek, recommend or hire them to work.

In the Amazonas state, most of the families realized late that they should ask for a better academic formation for their children, a phenomenon that spread around the half of the decade of 1990, along the higher volume of graduation degrees offered. However, in this period, the more relevant conditions to a degree or a good professional career went through a major change, being almost irrelevant the professional who seeks only a superior degree, or who have a degree in areas little explored by the job's market, just as those who cannot communicate in more than one language in a reasonable level. The technical knowledge aimed at more specific work processes changed the levels and exigencies to a higher-level job. The raise of minimum competences needed to have a good career imposed to all professionals of the modern age, said to be the information age, higher levels of investment in knowledge and education, given that the more restrict the work production, the service with higher aggregated value and the more distinguished the manipulation of highly accurate tools, the more elaborate and expensive the process of traversing it[17] (Hobsbawn 1994), raising the amount of investment to appropriate itself from such valuable knowledge, desired by the companies and the government.

Nonetheless, even considering as relevant the investment in intellectual capital, huge part of private investment aimed at Brazilian education still focus mainly in the higher education, and in courses who can produce immediately the highest amount of financial return. While in the Primary and Secondary Education the percentage of students in the private sector goes at little above 10%, in the Higher Education this percentage reaches almost 75%. Many factors could explain this, the main being the possibility of finding a reasonably better paying job:

> On average across OECD countries, a tertiary graduate can expect to earn over 50% more than a person with an upper secondary education. In Brazil, this premium is 156%, the highest among all countries, and provides a solid incentive for completing higher levels of education.[18]

This situation, relative to the private investment in education mainly focused in the superior education, starts to quickly redirect to the earlier levels of educations, especially the Secondary, composed by students who will compete for the few posts in the countries' best public universities. Producing a promising market for institutions who can provide better qualification, graduating students more and more competitive for these purposes. Nonetheless, the number of students registered in public schools at this stage is only about 10% of the total of students, given that, as said before, *in Brazil, the large majority of students, from kindergarten to secondary, is registered in public institutions.* [19]

The dark side of this situation is that it could lead to an even weaker quality of the public schools, for two reasons. First, the loss of students with higher potential to the private schools, as a way to assure a better performance at the classificatory exams for the public universities. Second, even worse than the first one, is that the families of students issued from the private schools are, for the most part, middle class, possessing a higher pressure power, more capacity of mobilization and demand. The distance between these families and the public school tends to weaken the debate and the force needed to implement improvements that could contribute to the quality of the public school as it is offered by the government, enlarging the gap between public and private in our country and creating a situation where the best courses are exclusively attended by those who can afford it, and not who can learn more.

Decades ago, our parents believed (and where right about it) that formal education is the best way to progress in live and to build a specific career. Nowadays, formal education is just a basic condition to aspire a possible worker stability, after a job with or without a defined profession, being necessary other essential qualifications to adequate ourselves to the exigencies of the market, making possible for the more committed professionals to compete for the best spots available in the labor market and be needed by both public and private institutions. And this perception that something more is needed made possible the creation of an infinity of extra-curricular "mandatory" courses like English for foreigners, or German, or Mandarin, or dance, music, coaching, MBA, negotiation techniques, business management, risk management, informational technology or any other course that can relate to the areas of most graduated professionals, including meditation techniques and extra-sensorial communication (if that's even a thing...)

Long ago, many discussions took place about the essential necessity that the professionals should recycle himself, in a continuous process in the same area. Today, besides the same-area courses being no longer a necessity, the term "recycle" became a swearing in the business world, as the recycled product is often of an inferior quality to the original. Soon, for the people focused on the new conditions of knowledge, "recycling" is not a process that can lead someone to the top, but actually lowering their positions. Because knowledge, being intellectual capital, is so expansive that it does not recycle, it just amplifies continuously. Knowledge expands itself through new ways of knowing and researching that leads to new information, while the recycled materials usually loses its main traits. Thus, today "recycling" is barely talked about, losing preference for reflexivity and expansion, meaning whatever that someone can aggregate to its basis of knowledge through learning, reanalysis, reading, experience, failure and acquisition of continual information, that can help to amplify the possibility of comprehension of the work process that someone can perform along their career or personal life.

In conclusion, the overrating of intellectual capital in the modern world, allied to the near bankruptcy of Brazilian public educational system and rising amount of competitiveness for places in the most promising courses of the best universities is leading more families in the country to invest by their own on basic education, extension and technological sapience in order to assure their children still competitive to the better paying jobs anywhere in the world. Besides, investing in acquisition of knowledge make possible that, in case they opt for building careers outside the formal labor market through entrepreneurship, they can put themselves ahead of other competitors in markets who require an above-the-average intellectual or economical capital.

The Society of Math's Knowledge

Currently, most of the applied research models, the main theoretical formulations, the methodological basic conditions and scientific conclusions are written mainly in mathematical language, or in a system based and ruled by it, like the operational systems-based reading, storage, manipulation, analysis and synthesis of data. The accurate mathematical language and reading is determining and essential to the operations of the main process and work methods typical of the Financial Sector worldwide. One of the main sectors of global economy and an essential ally to whoever needs financial support to product more, to those who want to get into the stock markets, derivative market, future market, hedge or simply the tax evasion market.

Among many forms of applications and practical usages of mathematics' considerations, the game theory, statistics and risk measuring seen to have a distinct appeal to governments and companies who works with data management, whose main functionality is to produce revenue and economic knowledge after the analysis of countless intertwined numerical variables. Currently, the game theory has been indeed relevant to many companies who seek to be more efficient, competitive, rational or simply take market advantage of the technical deficit, of the lack of accurate intel or operational fragility of their consumers.

Since the publishing of the work "Theory of Games and Economy Behavior" in 1944, by the great scientist Von Neumann along the economist Oskar Morgenstern, this different model of analysis was gradually gaining ground among researchers interested in studying the behavior of individuals in interaction with others, trying to find rational strategies in situations where the result depends, among other things, on the strategy chose by the other agents that may have different strategies to achieve a common goal[20]. More and more companies and governments try to utilize this theory to build strategical situations that could award them some advantage over the other agents that play the same "game" in all areas of knowledge, from modern political science to military arts. Nonetheless, it is in the economic area that most of the works about the game theory has been produced, including the award of a Nobel Prize in Economy to the brilliant American mathematic John Nash, for his huge contribution on researches destined to the improvement of this theoretical field.

One of the main goals of this theory is to analyze, size and guide decisions made by people or companies, which would be the best response to decisions made by other agents with a common interest in a given situation, coordinately producing the actions that could lead to the best result for one or both parts over the totality of the possible outcomes. One of the its fundamental considerations is to be able to anticipate the actions that would be most efficiently possible in relation to the total number of probable actions, considering the weight of the other variables and the strategic actions of the other agents in a situation where there are conflicts of strategies and results. Thus, this type of "comparative" analysis, on a mathematical basis, aiming to build actions and expected results on a given situation, has been widely used by many companies, in many situations that the prior knowledge of the reaction of other agents may produce some material or financial gain, including the possibility of evasion of taxes required by the State.

Imagine the following hypothesis: part of the economical agents that pay taxes in Brazil seen to realize the government has been systematically conducting special installment plans to the taxpayers owing the national treasure. These special installments have longer deadlines to their retarded pay off, diminishing of the interest rate or the possibility of taking maximum advantage of fiscal losses in payment, for interest and fine. Among all the legal possibilities, one of the installments recently granted by the federal government has the following traits:

> The debt that this law is about can be paid immediately with the deduction of 100% of interest default interest rate and fine, 40% for of the fines alone, 45% of the default interest and fine and 100% of legal legal charges.

That means that the taxpayer that correctly declare the values owed to the national treasury, but have not yet effected the payment of the sum owed could pay off their debts by the value properly declared, plus 55% of monetary adjustment, corrected by the monthly interest basic rate. To the taxpayers that evade tax information, but were framed by the monetary surveillance before the law was enacted, could also pay off their obligations in the same way, reducing by 100% the value of the applied fines (both default and legal penalty for trying to evade taxes).

The governments collect the financial resources needed to the realization of its daily activities, like paying the staff, investing in infrastructure, covering expenses with healthcare and education, mainly through charging taxes and selling government bonds at the financial market, or the receipt for the concession of exclusive activities by public companies.

Taxation and government bond selling are the main sources of revenue by the government. The compensation for the payment of tributary receipts obligatory charged from the citizens should be the offering of quality public services, while the compensation for the revenue obtained by credit operations is the payment of interest rate over the value of titles acquired by the families and companies who invest in this modality. Among the variety of options of government bonds the State display for negotiation, there is the SELIC (stands for "Special System of Offset and Custody", in Brazilian Portuguese) treasure, composed by negotiated titles whose interest rate payment is bound to the cumulated SELIC tax, a financial index for the update of receipts and expenses of the federal government. In 2016 the value of these titles in public possession were around R$ 209 billion, representing almost 8% of the national negotiated titles.

After acquiring these titles, the investor can receive the main value applied in its acquisition, plus the interest rate applied of the applied period, corrected by the SELIC tax, deducted of the income tax over the cumulated interest rate over the profit. The percentage of tax income is inversely proportional to the application period, fixing in between 27.5% for the shortest period and 15% for the longest period invested.

Supposing that a given company, whose directors have some understanding of the game theory and risk management, is willing to invest in the purchase of government bonds, on modality of SELIC treasure, in the year of 2010, with the value of R$ 10 million, to rescue its profit in five years. After this period, the company would be obliged to effect the rescue of its investment and think what to do with the profit.

Assuming the cumulated SELIC rate was around 49% and ignoring the period's inflation, the company would have in the act of rescue of investment, the net income of R$ 4.165 million – R$ 4.9 million minus the 15% of the deducted value of income tax. On the rescue act, the company shall receive R$ 14.165 million for their investment.

Let us consider that this same company, in 2010, owed R$ 12 million in taxes to the federal government. The directing board of the company shamelessly decided to pay only R$ 2 million and invest the rest on the government's own titles, as showed above, hoping to obtain some profit over the non-payment of the due taxes. On the year of rescuing of the applied values, the government enacted a law of special installments with the same traits of the previous law, which prevented interest and tax deduction to offset payment. Thus, the R$ 10 million that were not levied by the government in 2010 built up to the amount of R$ 16.867 million in 2015, being around R$ 2 million in default tax and R$ 4.867 in interest rate.

In the same year, the company expected to receive a sum for the government bonds it bought from the State, summing R$ 14.165 million. On the other hand, it would have a tributary tax of around R$ 16. 867 million, resulting on a deficit for evasion of R$ 2.702 million.

Analyzing the cold data, it was a terrible business to evade the due taxes and invest on the government's own titles. However, by enacting the law that reduces in 100% the default taxes and in 45% the interest rates, the company's debt would have been shortened by R$ 4.190 million, summing up to only R$ 12. 677 million. For the new configuration, processing the reductions, the company would still have the net profit of R$ 1.488 million to receive from the government itself, for the buyout of government bonds with the resources the company evaded taxes to gather – in other words, using the government's own money. In such conditions, the company would pay off its debt and would even profit freely almost R$ 1.5 million, for the right bet in considering that in a near future, a new installment rate law would be enacted, reducing interest rate and taxes.

This is nothing but a real example of how the Knowledge Society organizes, after the mathematical analysis, countless possibilities and situations that could offer real financial profit by, in this scenario, anticipating the actions the government could take, analyzing the risk and considering that the rationality of the system would help building a favorable situation for the decision it took: being the government's own creditor, by negating its taxes. Unfortunately, in many countries whose tributary structures fall short of the modern economic structures in terms of resources, management, qualified personnel and information processing, it is possible to find a structural system of tax evasion in a programmed, schematized and even monetized manner, aiming not only at the non-payment of its tributary duty, but at the use of advanced mathematical knowledge to shamelessly profit over the State.

To understand the magnitude of the giant market of tax evasion in Brazil, in 2015, the total value tributary credit inscribed in the Union's Active Debt summed over R$ 1 trillion. If we consider that only 10% of the debtors have an amount of understanding of the Game Theory, and they decide to gamble the government via risk management by letting go on their tributary duties to invest on the government bonds market, it is possible to state that in five years the net profit produced by the evasion would be around R$ 40 million, supposing the initial R$ 100 billion used to apply the public debt bonds would be collected after the investment rescue, otherwise the damage could be even worse.

This value matches around 65% of the Federal budget to the country's public education in 2017, and represents a considerable amount to any area the State wishes to invest in or expand the access. In addition to this value, there are still R$ 1 trillion tributary credits, confessed, owed, and non-collected, that the State could not receive for several reasons. Among these reasons, it is the high level of mathematical and law knowledge of the best professionals of the companies that owe huge amounts to the government, who can calculate at minimum risks the tax evasion and have the technical knowledge of "juridical loopholes" of the tributary law, making easier for the tax payer to refuse to pay the exact amounts of due tributes in the legal set dates and conditions imposed by those who have the power to charge taxes.

The Society of Mathematical Knowledge is highly advanced, selective and structure for several goals, can produce wealth through logical combination of data the processing of information gathered in many areas of knowledge, where the capacity to run models and specific rules of operation is a difficult task for most people who have no ease or conditions to appropriate themselves of numerical data reading and interpretation. Those who propose themselves such a task can feel like on the song "Want" by The Cure – but instead of singing "I want", like on the lyrics, they can sing "I can make".

> I want the sky to fall in
> I want lightning and thunder
> I want blood instead of rain
> I want the world to make me wonder
> I want to walk on water, take a trip to the moon
> Give me all this and give me it soon

Integral Knowledge and its new Scribes

The German historian Oswald Spengler stated that a new era had begun, where the scholar in which the scholar, the artist, the seer and the saint were replaced by the soldier, the engineer and the politician, resulting in a technical civilization[22] (GEERING, 1999). A technical civilization's main trait is the valuing of ideas, tools, proceedings and innovations built for its improvement of technological intervention in almost every area: from the educational process to the hydrogen bomb. Being necessary for such, the convergence of talented professionals, unusually skilled with the available resources, public or private, with major economical, strategical or negotiating skills, to invest in the creation of new technologies that can enable the expansion of knowledge levels and its rational application. In this aspect, the essence of the overrated knowledge in the modern world is under the conditions of the scientific method of investigation, based mainly in the knowledge that cannot be acquired through everyday experience, nor practiced or comprehended without many years of schooling[23] (Bourdieu, 2001) and hard work, research, intellectual development or a rational coordinated structuration.

For a long time in history, humankind produced diverse systems of symbolic communications, used for many ends and aimed at registering facts, acts and happenings, or just to stock commercial, legal and religious information, as well as establish laws and restrictions imposed by the ruler class to its vassals, beyond the already established rules of parenthood. The first Scribes, who knew the composition of the written symbols that bestow meaning to things, used to register their signs in clay, in a similar manner of the farmer who sown the soil for the plantation, as both had the earth as their main source of income. So, both had a similar disposition to interpret reality after their interaction with the everyday jobs on their fields. After the recording of signs in clay tablets, the written communication evolved to a modern abstract, symbolic communication, and currently is in such an advanced state that the main forms of writing and communication are through the prevailing system of material life production: the informational systems developed after an advanced computational basis.

As aforementioned, math is one of the main support basis of most modern sciences, and regarding the logical and computational systems, it is even more important to its structural development, aligned to the high creativity and visionary capacity of a few individuals who develop innovative products and services. Their main target is to offer simple solutions to everyday problems, like the countless apps and software used by millions of people around the world, serving as an essential tool to the organization of finances, traffic orientation, weather forecasting, information and communication with other systems subscribed under the same technological basis.

The first attempts of computational system development targeted, indeed, the possibility of simplification of complex mathematical calculations, in such way that ever since math would have a central position in the creation of every instruction that could allow the logical system to perform their functions. Still in 1640, the mathematician Blaise Pascal created a mechanical calculator to simplify his father's labor as a tax supervisor, being the first commercialized calculator ever, substituting the use of abacus as the main mechanism of mathematical calculation. Two centuries later, Charles Babbage took advantage of Pascal's invention and developed his own Difference Engine[24] (ISAACSON, 2014), aimed at simplifying polynomial functions and complex differential equations, through Vannevar Bush's Differential Analyzer, peaking at the development of ENIAC, considered the first modern age computational mechanism, constituted by its main resources and minimal conditions to be known as a computer.

The introduction of computational systems in the everyday activities of the determining structures of life in society consists in one more stage of the process of developing the means that make management, analysis and processing of data and information simpler, more trustworthy and structured for the aims it proposes. The symbolic written communication through letters and numbers were the knowledge of a few individuals along history, and were fundamental for the growth and improvement of material conditions to the human existence. Even though appearing on the old Mesopotamia thousands of years ago, the written communication remained exclusive to a few men during most of this time. Languages and writing system born, developed and ceased to exist without most of their native speakers being able to identify one single letter or form a short word through the elements of symbolic composition. The oral transmissions of knowledge was widely used through history, mainly because most individuals could not understand the communication via engraved, drawn or written symbols, produced only for the limited information trade between few citizens, government employees and the monocratic government itself, needed to create means of controlling its citizens, vassals and property, to better administrate production, stock and, mostly, taxation, over economic trades, which came to be normal in those ancient societies. This situation begun to revert mostly after the needs of the Catholic Church of graduating priests, missionaries and nuns for the preaching of the gospels of the catholic canon, through the structured teaching in monasteries, covens and universities. However, this educational structure were excluding and aimed mainly at the theological studies, in such manner that formal secular educational systems formed upon scientific basis would only be expanded with the huge propulsion of the industrial revolution, helping the rise of an educated worker's middle class, who knew how to read and write and had begun to communicate massively through written words, resulting in the construction of the postal mail systems, telegraphs and libraries, making possible for many writers the rise of a new mass market to consume their works, in a scale never before seen in western civilization.

In his most prominent work, Max Weber asserts that the birth of European Protestantism was essential for the growth of the literary production and the economic development of some countries, as the religious leaders encouraged their followers to read the Christian Bible. Ever since Martin Luther had begun to be translated from Latin into modern Indo-European languages, the need to learn how to read and write became popular, so no one would have to submit under an authority to interpret the Scriptures from its literal text. It contributed to the expansion of an even bigger market for authors and publishing works, especially in the central European countries whose literary production was massive.

Nowadays, the simple skills of reading and writing through conventional means are not enough to perform adequately specific functions, since the dominant modern writing is not only more complex and elaborate through a formal system known as "standard norm", but also requires abstract mathematical descriptions or some sort of link associated with it through specific symbols or coded computational language. Beyond the difficulty in reading and understanding, they yet produce high-value ideals in advanced theoretical ideals that often ignore traditional understanding, considering that many people have a "hard time digesting modern science because its mathematical language is difficult for our minds to grasp, and its findings often contradict common sense"[25] (HARARI, 2015).

This new systems of communication through symbols have acquired more and more importance and, in many cases, have put themselves as the main source of education and information. Mathematical language does not only materializes itself as computational systems or quantic physics, but also by collecting, analyzing and processing data, which allows the government, the companies and the professionals to build specific situations in complex structures, that can condition the efficient running of any organization's processes, which allied with the main process of processing knowledge in the modern age (the scientific one), is deeply rooted in schemed mathematical constructions.

Besides the mathematical language present in texts and modern codes, there is also the graphical language of the computational systems, which possibilities the interaction between the computer's network and those who utilize it, composed by schemed rules and conditioned by other sources. In a sense, considering that modern computers, text and video editors, calculation tabs, instructions for accurate analysis and other operations that allows the interaction between user and machine, follow a very distinct structure from the traditional means of reading. We can assume that there really is, in every society, the lack of people who can perform a proper interaction with the computer's language and without means to use any computational tool as a way to perfect knowledge, work and the life itself, constituting the individuals referred as digital illiterates.

Unfortunately, the term "digital illiterate" suggests a situation where people with formal education in how to learn and write and are able to interpret a written work but cannot interact properly with computational systems present in the offices or everyday houses, simply because those systems follow a different linguistic pattern from the system we currently use on traditional written communication. This situation puts those who have a hard time in reading and interacting with computational systems in an even worse life's condition, because the modern life, particularly in the professional life, consists mostly in the wide possibility of interventions resulting in the use of computers and logic systems in the most relevant aspects of rational functionality, excluding or pushing away people from many opportunities for the lack of adequate means of reading the modern code.

Thus, beyond every urgent matter the modern world demands from those who seek to keep updated on the dispute for the best posts in private companies or governments, a correct comprehension and reading of computational language a is fundamental and unavoidable, be it for the interaction with this systems or their improvement. In a sense, the "modern Scribes", those who are those able to read and redact the main norms and instructions needed for the performance of computer systems (hackers or programmers), has produced an unusual fascination over society, especially at the youngest who search earlier to comprehend the fundamentals of the logical complex systems. As many other, they try to learn prematurely how to design those mechanisms who serves as a base for the development of the computational autonomy.

Such situations has been producing a few interesting phenomena, changing the way we perceive formal education as the main factor of personal and professional growth, an established concept for the past generations, given that nowadays many bright young minds can accurately "talk" to the logical bases that fundaments computers and data processing. These young people are no longer committed to engaging a Master's or Doctor's Degree, simply about fame as a result of designing software and apps shared by countless users around the world, that could grant such designers a huge fortune even without academic titles. Probably after the notorious deeds and financial success of Bill Gates, his partners, and his god-like rival, Steve Jobs, many youngsters are seriously considering the development of systems, apps and software that could reward them a considerate wealth over worrying about competitive degrees of traditional superior education. Modern literature offers plenty of biographies of young talents that changed history, became millionaires or famous worldwide without having to worry about any sort of degree, as many of the first people dedicated to this activity were just "hippies, Whole Earthers, community organizers or hackers"[26] (ISAACSON, 2014) who would launch the new industry of personal computers and change the way we live and work, forever.

Furthermore, countless startups were created aiming the financing of ideas destined at the developments of computational systems or technological solutions of a high commercial value. In 2016, the value of investments in this niche were of the order of 16 billion dollars, of which 80% were the investment of the USA and China. The nest of the technology companies, the Silicon Valley, has over 20 thousand startup that, along the main companies in the region, sums up to 2 trillion American dollars, an amount superior to the GDP of most countries (including Brazil). It makes possible for this giant sector of logical technology to attract talented people, who want to settle among the countless opportunities of intellectual jobs, where the creation of inventive solutions can be highly profitable and can assure a good retirement even with a few years of work, something unthinkable a few decades ago.

Most of the talented people engaged in this process consider that degrees and specific careers are almost irrelevant in this niche market, considering that the main factor is the technical knowledge, the capacity of innovation and high amounts of creativity and disposition to work on something does not yet exist, after the combination of imagination, computer science and tireless work.

Another fundamental issue for the talents and "scribes" who seek to work in the development and operation of modern computational systems is the high level of security most databases require (particularly on the financial and military sectors), as they cannot be protected by traditional systems of security and surveillance created in the Antiquity to assure the protection of livestock and stocks of cumulated metals, tools and weapons that could be target of greed by other people. The logical systems of the modern age need essentially logical security, built on the same terms of what it intends to be protected from. Thus, the companies who work essentially with data and important information, especially of personal or financial order, and who needs to shield such data from anyone who intend to use it to achieve fame or money. Many companies invest heavily on those who can perceive and point out failures on their systems that could jeopardize their operations and business. Banks, credit operators, stockbrokers and governments are among the main targets of organized hackers who intend to practice cybercrimes, financial coups and kidnaping of data. The damage caused by cybercrime is has grown exponentially around the world, and according to a Juniper Network's study, "the rapid digitization of consumers' lives and enterprise records will increase the cost of data breaches to $2.1 trillion globally by 2019" [27], being that in 2015 the cost of cyber security around 70 billion dollars and has been growing at a rate of over 10% per year.

That way, it is possible to conclude there is sheer valorization of professionals that can read, copy, write and manipulate the "letters" that composes the alphabet were are "written" the main instructions and norms of the logical modern systems, as much as the old scribes of the past, especially those who recorder their versions of God and history in the pages of the Old Testament. Being those scribes instructed and patronized by kings and sovereigns, they shaped the customs, changed relations, subverted facts and built a world according to their ruler's visions through writing, materialized and available only to a small parcel of the elite they represented.

Nowadays, this cultured elite, protected and every day wealthier, is constituted the same way the former, through the appropriation of an indispensable specific resource: the capacity of reading and writing codes that feed the process of collecting, stocking, processing and manipulating encoded data, through the countless databanks around the world, scattered around the world in every area of knowledge. It undeniably produces a remarkable value for those who dream of the achieving financial "stardom", instead of dreaming of a master or doctor degree as the past generations.

This new scribes are building "laws" and instructions that condition life in society, in large and intertwined areas that it is almost possible to believe in a shared process of existence, where most people cannot realize that their lives depends more and more on technological constructions.

Referências Capítulo II

1. Fritjof Capra, **The Turning Point: Science, Society and the Rising Culture**, 2006, p. 28
2. Peter Drucker, **Men, Ideas and Politics**, 2012, p. 61
3. Walter Isaacson, **The Innovators: How a Group of Hackers, Geniuses and Geeks Created the Digital Revolution**, 2014, p. 309
4. Peter Drucker, **Men, Ideas and Politics**, 2012, p. 19.
5. Eric Hobsbawn, **The Age of Extremes: The Short Twentieth Century 1914-1991**, 1995, p. 329-330
6. www.millwardbrown.com/brandz/top-global-brands/2016
7. Nonaka e Takeuchi, **Knowledge Management**, 2008.
8. Yuval Noah Harari, **Homo Sapiens – A Brief History of Mankind**
9. Jacques Le Goff, **Medieval Calling.**
10. Geoffrey Blainey, **Short History of the World.**, p. 213.
11. Alvin Toffler, **The Third Wave**, 2010, p. 23
12. Yuval Noah Harari, **Homo Sapiens – A Brief History of Mankind**, p. 214
13. Alvin Toffler, **The Third Wave**, 2010, p. 39.
14. Yuval Noah Harari, **Homo Sapiens – A Brief History of Mankind**, 2015, p. 259
15. Eric Hobsbawn, **The Age of Extremes: The Short Twentieth Century 1914-1991**, 1994, p. 261
16. Ibidem, 296
17. Ibidem, 256
18. Brasil - Country Note - Education at a Glance 2015: OECD Indicators
19. Portal.mec.gov.br/component/tags/tag/32123
20. https://en.wikipedia.org/wiki/Game_theory
21. Brazilian Law 12.996/2014 - www.planalto.gov.br/ccivil
22. Lloyd Geering, **The World to Come: From Christian Past to Global**, 2011, p. 43.
23. Pierre Bourdieu, **Language & Symbolic Power**, 2001, p. 20
24. Walter Isaacson, **The Innovators: How a Group of Hackers, Geniuses and Geeks Created the Digital Revolution**
25. Yuval Noah Harari, **Homo Sapiens – A Brief History of Mankind**
26. Walter Isaacson, **The Innovators: How a Group of Hackers, Geniuses and Geeks Created the Digital Revolution**
http://www.jornaleconomico.sapo.pt em 06/06/2017.

> The roots of education are bitter, but its fruits are sweet.
> Aristotle

III – Education and Learning

The systems of education were built specifically for the instruction of arts, letters, numbers and science, and developed in societies where the skill of reading and writing were restricted to a small circle and most books were written in a different language, Greek or Latin. Only after the Industrial Revolution and the availability of massive educational systems to cover the demands of the rising production system was when the rates of illiteracy were gradually diminishing, after the western European countries. However, in this long process, other forms of communication and information were developed, becoming essential for the work and everyday situations, making the reading and writing skills no longer enough to comprehend the facts. In most of the everyday activities, reading and writing are only differentials if can be done in more than 2 languages, given that beyond the correct reading, there is now a huge need for the interpretation and communication through computational systems and logical technologies in every area. In this aspect, one of the country's major problems begins precisely at the limited capacity of reading of most of its population, whose only encouragement to learn to learn this basic skill as a way to get an eventual job, instead of learning how to think or to acquire knowledge and culture. The result is a generation of professionals whose deficit in interpretation, reading and writing extends to the efficient form of communication with machinery, tools and systems who require logical and computational systems.

Brazil, Education and Everything Else Late

The modern world consists in a structured, advanced system who creates, processes and moves information and knowledge in a global scale, along countless forms and technological systems destined at perfecting the work, communication and mass access to information, whose goal varies accordingly to the economic and social facts and the need to bridge the gaps between things and people. Nonetheless, even living in a world where most goals seem easy to achieve, many people suffer of a feeling of insufficiency, especially of objective information that can turn into knowledge, and knowledge that can turn into comfort, goals, dreams or anything that can enable a more pleasing existence.

The historical Brazil is a huge disappointment in terms of production of knowledge, where many people seek meaning in the alphabetical letters, whereas many dynamic countries find themselves years ahead of us in mathematical expression.

Along these five centuries, Brazil has been built after the agglutination of various retarding processes in every field of production, from education to democracy, from ecology to industrialization, where the limitations caused by an inefficient system of mass education resulted in one of the greatest losses for generations of Brazilians, and helped the maintenance of deficient political and economic structures.

Even though Portugal was ahead of the European nations regarding naval technology, it was nothing but a tiny country bound to the limits of Iberian Peninsula and ever since the exploitive colonization of our territories, every process of implantation an occidental society in this lands were conditioned by the metropolis' needs. Brazil was just a huge resource mass, available to exploitation and an undeniable property of Portuguese kings. The Portuguese nautical advances were followed by other technological advances developed in Europe at the time, were many tools (especially after the invention of the press), works and studies allowed an "update" of the technological basis inherited from the Middle Ages, followed by the gradual abandon of the biblical truths and the church's interpretation of facts and data, replacing it by rational explanations. Constituted by many men and women who dared to defy the truth of facts and engaged themselves in rewrite concepts after the point of view of humankind itself, after the utility of applied research, be it on humanities or natural sciences, or even spiritual sciences.

After a while, Portugal was eventually surpassed on the technological race flowering on the whole continent, and, the more limited Brazilian's product exploration became, the more hard to implement technological and basic knowledge who could enable to impulse any movement towards a the construction of a modern society, both in metropolis and in colonial Brazil. This capacity limitation would have devastating impact over Brazil and its future population, inheriting from Portugal a poor, rural country, largely illiterate and ruled by a hillbilly, corrupt and retrograde elite. Furthermore, the prohibition of slavery left thousands of former slaves on their own devices around the major cities, violently forbidden of studying in white people's schools, of working in the rising companies, of actively participating in political and cultural activities or of defining which values they should build after the recovery of their freedom.

The fall of the Portuguese government and the wave of independency movements in the Americas overthrew the Imperial monarchy and granted a fictional autonomy in Brazil, who started to administrate its own affairs without making a real change in the society's structures, neither in its law, political, educational or productive systems, nor in the class division. The next step to the independence was the change of its form of governments, changing the monarchy for a three-piece oligarchical republic through a military coup that sought to banish the last reminiscence of the Portuguese dominion. However, its implementation was without any popular participation, and again without any change on the political, economic and educational structure of the former colony, whose population remained largely rural, catholic, illiterate and underrepresented on the nation's decisions.

Regarding education, the historical of public investment remained meaningless and insufficient ever since the country's formation, aggravated by the fact that most of the population lived in the rural areas, far from the State's legal structures, with limited resources and under direct control of the land owners, making difficult to create a wide, solid educational system. The result was a rate of 75% of the Brazilian population being illiterate, and 73% on the Amazonas state, as state in the Geography and Statistics Brazilian Institute's (IBGE) annual report for the year of 1920[1].

The slow economic progress of the country, for the lack of interest by the rural elites and the awful conditions of the educational systems resulted in a slow fall on the rates of illiteracy, being around 62% by the 1940's[2].

The successive crisis on the coffee's price, national product of exportation who regulate the national GDP, just like the paralysis of the international markets during the first World War, the Wall Street Crash in 1929, and in a lesser degree, the fall of the Amazonia's rubber production. Those factors contributed to the diversification of the national small industrial circle, who started to produce internally products that used to be imported, initially using the European immigrant's labor, and producing food and shopping consumer goods.

In Amazonas, the situation became gradually worse due to the fall of the rubber production network, falling from a huge wealth to near misery, with a strong cut on the average income and the transfer of wealthier families to other region, loss of public revenue and immense debt from the ostentatious monuments during the jungle's Belle Époque.

Here, as elsewhere in the country, the construction of an industrial society would require a deep change of values, social organization, law's structure and quality of public institutions, given that industrial mass production demands workers technically prepared for a different realities than the Brazilian's manufacture or rural labor at the time, and the overwhelming majority of uneducated people in Brazil obstructed this model. With the fall of the Old Republic regime and the arrival or Getulio Vargas at the national political scenario in the decade of 1930, the economic elite was proven that illiteracy constituted a major limitation for country's development, and one of the measures adopted was the educational programs for young people and adults without formal education, for the first time a relevant issue on the national politics. In 1942, the federal government raised a specific fund who bound 25% of the educational resources to the education of adults, called FNEP.

> The creation of the FNEP in 1942, whose functioning would begin only in 1946, is considered the cornerstone of the public politics aimed at the education of adults, recognized into the spectrum of basic popular education.

The simple attempt of structuring a public efficient education, with limited resources, had little impact on most of the black and poor population of the country, to which only a fragile, basic education was available. Beyond that, the great mass of rural population, largely unassisted by public educational plans, would have to send their children to the closest towns in order to have them receive education of any sort. The years who followed up to the Vargas Age were wasted on behalf of political and economic feuds between the wealthy right wing and left wing politicians, instead of trying to promote expressive changes to make Brazil a wealthy, strong nation. However, to the national elites (who counted on every privilege to register their children on the best schools) the eradication of illiteracy only served the purpose of teaching how to read and write, and after several decades of insufficient efforts to correct the historical damage, the average rate of illiteracy were still of 24% in the decade of 1980, and 20% of the population above 10 years old in 1991.[4] In other words, in 60 years, between several coup d'état, the country could not lower the illiteracy rates under 2 digits, even though in 1934 the Federal Constitution instituted the obligational, universal access to the primary education after completed their 7 years. To have a broader idea of the Brazilian educational retard, in 1945, South Korean population was 88% illiterate, while Brazilian rate was of 56%. However, in 1961, the South Korea rate fell to 29%, while the developing Brazil was around 40%. A reduction of 70% of South Korean illiterates, against only 28% of Brazilian's. The brutal difference reflects also on the income rate of the average Brazilians and South Koreans nowadays.

By the end of the decade of 1980, Brazil went through a deep process of urbanization, which progressively left the rural areas and move towards the cities seeking better conditions, a process of overgrowth without basic conditions of education, security, sanitation and habitation for most of the immigrants, leading to the construction of favelas. In this period, the country attempted to amplify massively the public education, focusing on the basic and secondary education. Nonetheless, with a low supply of available qualified teachers, aligned with corrupt politicians and financial insufficiency led to a scrapping of the quality of the education, whose main goal was to teach only how to read and write. Meanwhile in the developed world, the educational qualifications were reinvented years before.

In this staggering route, the Higher Education had no additional incentive, and was promoted and kept mainly for the federal government through an insufficient number of institutions were thousands of students fought for the few available posts in the public universities, through the exhausting and exclusive vestibular exams. The expansion of universities is recent and mainly reposes on the offer of graduation courses by private institutions, conditioned by the external economic needs instead of the desire to build a savant society, conscious society given that:

> The politics of Higher Education have been justified by the undeniable changes promoted by the economic globalization, the dissemination of informational technology and the valuing of knowledge.[5]

Such expansion resulted from the paradigmatic inversion of the industrial societies, deep rooted on the idea of preparing workers for the operation of work tools, instead of graduating citizens prepared for life in society and for the composition of the governmental and social structures.

After decades of pointless efforts, when the Collor government decided to open the Brazilian market in the early decade of 1990, Brazil's inherited structures still reflected a population whose past was recently rural, a deeply broken partisan politics torn apart by the mad years of military dictatorship and a surprisingly late educational level who could not afford to receive the scientific, technologic and cultural novelties of the Information Age and the Globalization. When the country asserted itself openly on the global market, the educational and labor force deficit was overwhelming in contrast with other countries who struggled with the same conditions, and as a result, led to a perceived lack of talents and differential professionals in almost every area, making even more difficult for the country to compete effectively on the international market beyond a few agrarian traditional products. The modern structure caught off-guard a country unprepared to deal with the more relevant conditions of the global economy.

The lasting and general delay of the educational systems on the country produced a high damage on the country's structures, who seemed to have walked aimlessly in search of a green rich field to settle down and live peacefully, and by not finding it, settled down in a most agonizing way, spreading the ugliest aspects of a cultural and educational malformation through society, especially on the legal devices of power's legitimacy, the Republic itself, undeniably reflecting the defects of its own people.

At last, the need of building a strong, prosperous nation through an independent and nationalist process of industrial, open to the world's economy and propelled by the creation of a universal, modern educational system has yet to find enough support of the nation's economic and political elites. Brazil was kept on the back row for too long, adapting or restructuring to the process and systems developed and already stapled in other parts of the world, always late and in an unrefined manner. Only a few modernity embryos can be found, like the Butantã Institute, the National Institute for Research in the Amazonia (INPA) and the Brazilian Company of Researches in Agriculture-Husbandry (EMBRAPA), beyond a feel other colleges and polytechnic institutes who managed to keep above average and could graduate strong professionals, even though limited and unable to avoid the political games. For the national political system, the politics are private, particular needs and the huge bureaucratic machinery of the Brazilian State shuns down the needs of the population.

College Degree, at Any Cost

To have a Higher Education by any means available is an idea that developed in our country, mostly because of the supposition of better salaries and better jobs are bound to the possession of a college degree and despite most students not being sure about which area of knowledge combines more with their profile. People who believe in it seem to be studying only to achieve a degree and influenced by the mere conviction of a possibility, if not safe, at least with less riskier to find a job and have recognition, further constituting a solid path to the building of a career or a meaningful life. Nonetheless, they seem to forget that a Superior Degree means study, research and extension and serves mainly as a fundamental basis to amplifying knowledge and ameliorating the levels of work, security, health and comfort in a country.

The educational delay inherited from the past generations produced a huge hiatus between the necessity of graduating qualified professionals and the demands of the modern world for strengthening wealth, security and democratic institutions in a competitive environment focused in its production system and management of bases deeply linked to informational technology.

Between 2000 and 2010[6] in Brazil, the percentage of professionals who went through a Superior Education raised from 4.4% to 7.9%. Despite every effort and advances on the graduation courses, only 11% of the population over 24 years old had a degree in 2012, establishing at around 15% nowadays, an indeed low level for countries member of the G20 and the BRICS. It conditions and limits the level of productivity, damages the development of education and freezes the quantity and quality of the countries Intellectual Property, its base of scientific and technologic innovation with commercial, business or security ends.

According to the available data, the Brazilian worker shows one of the worst educational levels between the countries with most percentage of total wealth. The most part of the worker's level of education caps at around a complete high school, 31% in total. While professionals with college degree sums up to 16% in Brazil, the North Region falls short, showing only 10% of graduated workers.[7]

In most prosperous countries, the rate of population with a college degree is usually up to 40%. Comparing to the same percentage band, it is easily perceivable that Brazilian workers with a complete superior education is of less than half of most countries. Russia and Canada both have more than half their populations with a college degree. Japan, USA and South Korea, over 40%. In the rest of the central countries, mostly, the rate is above 30%.

For the state of the Amazonas, the last years have been of extraordinaire growth for students subscribed in graduation courses. According to the Map of the Higher Education in Brazil from 2015, in the period between 2000 and 2013, the rate of students grew around 459%. In 2013, Amazonas had 137 thousand students attending regular graduation courses, 84 thousand on the private sector and 53 thousand in the public network. Still, in 2013, there was over 11 thousand students attending distance courses.

According to the same report, there was 194 courses of regular graduation in 2000 in Amazonas, which increased to 659 in 2013, being 249 offered by private institutions. The numbers presented the courses of Law, Administration, Pedagogy, Nursing and Accounting as those who counted more attending students. This numbers are great when analyzed separately, however, in the same period, the rate of academic evasion was around 49%-52% in private schools, against 48% in the public system[9]. It can indicate diverse situations, as the lack of funding and resources for those who need scholarships, the eventual change of career focus, or simply the high rate of quitting can be traced down to the offering of obsolete courses with little to no relation to the practice field.

From the students who got into the universities in 2010, only 29% concluded the graduation in 2014, 21% are still attending and the rest, quit[10]. This date converge to the OECD's research which appointed that in Brazil around 20% of the young people under 29 years did not studied nor worked. This degreeless group have the tendency to the least favorite on the job's market, considering that most companies demand a basic formal education by the time of hiring and to keep studying even after obtaining a degree is a basic requisite to improve employability, income and stability.

Countless factors contribute to the evasion and lingering on graduation courses. Certainly, the low quality of the teaching can be one of those, just like difficulties in learning due to poor conditions in High School. Another factor can relate directly to the number of quitting or "repeating" is that most students of graduation courses choose to attend their course at night, around 60% according to the census of 2010[12].

Most students of the night shift attend their classes after accomplishing an exhausting daily work shift. Data from Datapopular Institute of 2012 points out that 70% of Brazilian college students also do work. This numbers indicate that at short-term, many students worry more about their current income than their graduation course, resulting in the evasion or simply the prolongation of the course.

Just like in any market, the superior degree title's market possess its degrees of valor and complexity, tending to be sought by companies and governments the closest the candidate is to the adequate level of formal education, despite those courses being highly expensive and way beyond the market's average rate. It clearly shows that in the country, there is an absurd gap between the graduation levels of college students regarding the same course in different public institutions, where some universities can offer advanced courses and graduate professionals, while other serve only as an extended version of high school. Furthermore, the huge disparity in superior education courses in different universities, both in graduation and post-graduation research programs, ends up disqualifying countless institutions and tends to turn useless or diminish the importance of thousands of students of the "suburban universities", creating a market of graduated professionals with no jobs nor careers. There are even those who take up jobs that do not fit their formal education, producing even a professional with several unrelated degrees, attending different courses according to the needs of the companies they work for, without a glimpse of talent for a career or trying to compete for the ranks of public administration servant through competitive public tests.

In Amazonas, even after the spurts of college educated professionals, there are still a lack of specific requirements to assume some roles. As a response, a large market of lato sensu graduate courses sprouted, with repetitive contents whose importance fits only on the job's market, to the point where most offered courses are demanded by organizations, not including the research and expansion a Master's or a Doctor's degree could offer.

It is possible to assert even that most post-grad courses offered by the private network do not make available studies about the specificities of the amazon region, or about its base of its already existing real knowledge, confirming that the contents worked in such institutions often are imported from anywhere else in the world. Although not necessarily bad, it can often limit the opportunities of constructing and spreading local knowledge, or even, in absurd situations, scramble or mock the knowledge the inhabitants try to preserve. It is the case of the pink river dolphin, who only came to inhabit the amazon's fauna by mere ignorance of those who "discovered" them alive, without any experience or commitment with the Amazon's culture and history. However, while the systems of knowledge production does not prioritizes Amazon, it is clear that the studies about the region are being conducted more often by international institutions, and the contribution of amazonenses scientists is nearly null or barely noticeable, in an irreversible process of transferring the exploration of unique knowledge.

In any case, even though the high demand for a higher education degree is aimed at the acquisition of formal education essential to assure or improve the employability, in many cases this assumption has been proved wrong, given that Brazil still has one of the lowest rates of job productivity among the industrialized countries and many companies would rather invest in other parts of the world than hiring more general professionals. This tendency is being particularly proven by the progressive migration to automatic systems, producing a generation of individuals who started to realize a certain advance of a perverted system who educated for the unemployment.

Failed Education, Bad Productivity

The level of knowledge any society aims to achieve imposes a certain need for sacrifices and ordeals needed to the formation of people and construction of supporting structures for its process, and the biggest institutional sacrifice is the finances needed for the creation, maintenance and expansion of a modern, efficient educational system. In Brazil, this model has yet to find a reliable ground to build upon, as reflected in its immediate problems such as the Brazilian worker's pace of production, perceivably slower than in other countries with a similar productive configuration.

Historically, the less educated Brazilian worker was always inefficient and advanced almost nothing towards the levels of comparative work's productivity. As the Brazilian magazine *Exame* published, in September 2013:

> Brazil lost eight positions and settled at 56th position of work's productivity, among 148 studied and its fall was ascribed to the lack of tributary and structural reforms, among others. The Latin-American region is continuously affected by the fragile work of institutions, infrastructure and inefficiency of assigning production's factors,

accordingly the WEF communicate. This is the result of an "insufficient level of competitiveness and a gap in instruction and formation terms, technology and innovation development, impeding many companies of advancing to higher-stake activities".[14]

Another site, in an October 2015 article, concludes an analysis over the lack of productivity in the country as such:

> Brazil lost eighteen more positions in the ranking of the world's most competitive economies, falling to the 75th position according to the World Competitiveness Report, revealed by the World's Economic Forum (WEF) this Tuesday in a partnership with Dom Cabral Foundation. The Report asserts that Brazilian economy suffers with the deterioration of basic competitiveness factors, such as trust in Institutions, public accounting deficits and factors of business sophistication, as the ability to innovate its education.[15]

In both analysis, the bad educational factor and weak professional capacitation posed major roles for the labor force's low level of production and low competitiveness of Brazilian companies. Considering the actual level of production possess an important correlation with the level of education and capacitation, it indicates that the national industry still presents little innovation and a weak development of production techniques, impeding an improvement in the rate of current productivity. Besides, many of the foreign companies that settled in Brazil possess their own advanced technologies, whose necessity for actual labor force is indeed restrict, making almost no contributions on the productivity pace.

One of the central problems of the national worker's low productivity starts certainly by its inadequate formation, technically deficient for most professionals, historical consequence of a delayed, inefficient education who limits access to efficient, modern tools, like the computational means, as portrayed earlier in this book. As such, the growing computerization of the means of production, work and management was not aligned with a technical formation regarding the use of these tools essentially aimed at improving productivity in a production chain. Synthetizing, it appears to have a hiatus between the basic knowledge of the Brazilian worker and the technological availability of modern economy, limiting the capacity of innovation and introduction of new improvements. Considering that many companies display modern, secure computational systems available for their collaborators, although not plainly used at its full capacities, something that for many people may seem difficult to understand since:

> Most observers believe that the information economics and the strength of informatics has been giving an impulse in global economy simulator to the one produced by steam power, electric and oil energy in the past. (...). Some argue that it is hard to obtain convincing proof that computers accelerate significantly the rates of economic growth and production. [16]

This duality of positions relates mainly to the operational conditions that professionals develop in the process of work involving a differential use of computational systems, tending to proportionate a higher level of productivity, not only according to the availability of new technologies but mainly in their use after each worker's personal skill of correct reading its instructions and a collective of aptitudes acquired through interaction in the productive process.

Theses computational systems possess a specific language and does not uses standard models of user interaction, needing additional reading and operationalization for its correct use in tasks execution. One of the main difficulties Brazilian workers present regarding this correct reading is due to their bad basic or even academic formation, especially when it comes to math, English and Portuguese, which would be fundamental for the correct operation of equipment who uses different, often foreign systems of reading and interaction. The difficulties of operating any tool raise the level of stress and demotivate the professionals to perfect they work safely and efficiently, which can significantly raise the production costs of a good, considering that the necessary time to produce goods can be a measure of the company's operational costs.

Another important issue is the company's expressive cost of acquisition of advanced technologies, who tends to mitigate it through its productive chain, raising the production by unity or by worker (marginal product), cutting the production's necessary time, resulting in the cut of additional costs to the process, like energy consumption. When professionals can no longer keep up with the acquisition more advanced technologies, the costs tend to rise instead of lowering, summing up to the stress of the collaborators and the waste of limited resources, resulting in the diminishing of the financial return of applied investment, the part of the profit that would allow the company to distribute among their investors or apply more in productive investments.

It is common hearing about the "Brazil Cost" as a limit to the level of investment in the country or in specific regions. However, this visible Brazil Cost, which raises the costs of companies in the process of production due to the lack of structure in the harbors, transportation, government bureaucracy, high taxes, also related to the insufficiency of professionals in a wide array of areas, especially technological, management and talents formation, which became essential tools to the global scale competitiveness. It is impossible to openly import such professionals neither force their formation through specific laws. Grooming talents takes time, energy, organization and lots of money, and each stage in their formation serves as an essential basis for their future trainings. It is undeniable that the poor level of productivity of the Brazilian worker is at least in part due to the bad level of education inherited from the past generations, of the negligence regarding the level of a knowledge basis and the delayed chain of social learning that lingers in our country, being perhaps the most expensive part of the "Brazil Cost".

The Duty of Raising and Nourishing Knowledge

The final product in the process of education necessarily is to enable the socialization of the relevant and essential knowledges, determining the expansion of knowledge cumulated in the past. It precisely begins when we perceive that our basis of knowledge about existence, about life's phenomena, about production, about ideas, about laws of the universe and of society, about the systems of that keep the planet alive, are all insufficient and limited. Besides, the problems related to the forms of family unit, group participation and the relationships between countries constantly conflicts with new ways of how individuals and institutions work, act and think, demanding constantly new researches and updated knowledge which allow humankind, companies and countries to remain in peace, conscious of their responsibilities to each other, the planet and whatever they intend to build for themselves.

Every conscious learning process allows the man to gather and expand knowledge that enables a better existence with himself and the others, considering that for companies and governments, knowledge became the more important factor of competitiveness, essential to building and improving products, services, and solutions to ease people's lives through clean, cheap and efficient productive process. Cumulated knowledge needs to aim a specific end, and for being considered an advanced competitiveness factor, became primordial in the modern systems of production, management and control, making possible to obtain more efficiency and safety in the governments and companies' operational process, while still being able to develop this systems through technological systems and resources.

Modern pedagogy tries to bring individual's level of knowledge closer together through a reflexive educational process built upon the basic values of the learner instead of the teacher. Nonetheless, in every level of education, the appropriation of knowledge is different between people, through multiple tools of learning socialization, built along their social and genetic existence. The expansion of knowledge needs as many committed people as it needs a methodological basis which can "forge" in people the necessity to push further, regarding the progressive "packages" of socially built knowledge. In this scenario, people, countries and companies that historically cumulated more knowledge tend to remain ahead of the others in the race for the economic amplification and exploitation of the net product of their own differential appropriation. The so-called central countries structure their productive chain, government and social relations strongly around human capital and advanced logic systems, unlike latecomers like Brazil, who even though investing in means of self-promotion, would hardly be able to mitigate the cumulated distance between the more developed countries.

The educational systems have been turning more and more complex, while the pace of knowledge also applies to the same dynamics of its production. This founds a growing movement of private financial resources injected directly in educational quality, especially because of the bankruptcy and downfall of public educational systems.

The public expenses with education in Brazil consumes a substantial part of government's resources, and when we divide the total cost by the quantity of students, the country stands far from the world's most developed countries, as the OECD'S average per student is of almost 9 thousand USD, while the Brazilian government spends less than 3 thousand USD per student. As a result, many Brazilian families' expenses with private-sector education grew, reaching around 55 billion reais last decade. [17]

Besides the insufficient financial resources spent per student, Brazil still has an even bigger deficit in investments needed for the improvement of education professionals, especially the pedagogical improvement needed for the utilization of new technologies who could aid the process of teaching and learning, since, regarding the technological resources used in the teaching process, the rapport points out that Brazil provides one personal computer for every 22 students, while OCDE'S average is of 5 students. To make it even worse:

> Around 27% of the teachers on the final years of middle school declare to have a high degree of necessity of professional development in teaching with IT, and circa 37% declare to have a necessity of professional development with IT in the workspace.[18]

The difficulty presented by the teachers is profoundly damaging to the whole educational process, as knowledge is shared through systems organized by people, and inefficiencies presented by teachers tend to linger and spread all along the educational cycle: from basic education to Graduate School, through various mechanisms, being the *socialization* the more used in the public systems of education, *which is a process of sharing experiences and, as such, creating knowledge*[19], centered around a specific subject of acquired knowledge. This process became deeply damaging when verified that deficient socialization begins exactly since the ones who could not acquire enough knowledge to be able to teach, reproduced all along the system through badly prepared and demotivated teachers.

Socialization, when built upon adequate, efficient foundations, is essential to the investigation of relevant educational questions, as it is the main vehicle of knowledge transmission via reading, interpretation and exposition. After a process of externalization, it is possible to articulate *subtle knowledge in explicit concepts (...) taking the form of metaphors, analogies, concepts, hypothesis or models*[20], who can be compared, reproduced and amplified inside a continuous, coordinate process, whose end is necessarily the collective learning of the upcoming generations who will expand this knowledge. We must consider that socializing knowledge through a continuous process of learning is the more adequate path, the quintessence of creating structural knowledge[21] whose main goal is the process of every country's formal educational program.

Unfortunately, Brazilian public schools are largely late regarding the programmatic contents, methodology and pedagogical tools essential to producing knowledge nowadays. Where talented students are often too discriminated or induced to give up on their innovative aptitudes and their creative ideas for not caring enough for the routine, ritualized teaching of math and chemistry, for instance. Brazilian schools are usually unappealing to individual creativity, spending too much focus on the content's acquisition, where those who think differently are bullied into staying silent and obedient to the Master of the Puppets, just like in the fantastic song by Metallica on their most creative, homonymous album.

This alarming situation takes place in a moment of human history where the main professional requirements are creativity, capacity of being different and motivation for innovation. As a result, most of the young students who are trying hard on classes are losing their abilities of being different and creative thanks to the Brazilian educational deficits, systematically leading to the shrinking of many bright minds and limiting careers that, in other contexts, could be huge, if conducted by "educators" who could reinforce their own learning and pass it on, outside of the educational formal system.

The deficient, limiting routine of the public-sector teaching in Brazil, regarding the creative capacities of modern students, among many considerations and concepts that may be explored, allows for a reinforced comprehension of what is inequality in the levels of human and economic development. In more developed countries, it relates more with the gap in knowledge appropriation than any other factor, given that separates developed countries from the others is not only a gap in natural resources, but an abyss in knowledge (NONAKA, TAKEUCHI, 2008)[22]. For the despair of thousands of Brazilian students, this new world is being built exactly upon a remarkable basis of cumulated knowledge, especially the ones with immediate economic application, materializing through a modern system of institutional learning, and researches whose main goal is to generate more resources for the application of new researches and discoveries, making this cyclic investment dynamics the most important tool in the modern age, and fundamental condition to differ the level of prosperity between people, countries and companies. Those who find themselves late are indeed those who could not understand the perverse meaning of the amazing song Master of Puppets, pointing out precisely how many "masters" and "managers" conduct their students and partners all over Brazil.

> Master of puppets, I'm pulling your strings
> Twisting your mind and smashing your dreams
> Blinded by me, you can't see a thing
> Just call my name 'cause I'll hear you scream
> Master.... Master

Rebuilding a Country Through Education

How to build an idea, a family or a country without ethical, structural system of teaching and learning? How to clear the image of the public school system and endow it with a sense of collective belonging, a central resource in the process of building this very society?
How to socialize the comprehension that public schools are also a living organism, of superior importance to life in society? And how to make this organism healthy? Those are the main questions that we need to respond before trying to rebuild a country morally and materially wrecked.

This affirmation sounds quite pessimistic but, time after time, after the divulgation of data referring to Brazilian education, most communication means elaborate critical comments about the problems of teaching in Brazil, where only a few can effectively describe what happens in the public teaching and what could be the general solutions adequate to the improvement of the educational system. It is necessary to consider that the actual system has already around 30 years of delay and failure, and suffered so many clueless, disconnected attempts of improvement that it would be indeed difficult to build it after a single standard model. Besides there are huge distortions between public schools themselves, reflecting the model of spatial distribution of income, concentrating in the poorest and more isolated zones of the country the majority of those who present the worst statistical performance in middle and high school.

Public teaching in Brazil concentrates the majority of students, always presented late contents, is poorly managed and victim of violent misappropriation of public funds by public agents and less-than-noble managers. Even since Vargas Age, where education became a public duty and a universal right (despite few exceptions), the quality of public teaching was never ahead the political priorities nor do the wishes of the national elite, who tended to always send their own children to study abroad. Another relevant point, which directly affected Brazilian student's level of learning, is the lack of commitment of the family with the learning process. In Brazil, most of the families consider that education is still a State-only responsibility, exclusively offered by it, and thus avoids getting involved with extra-classes activities or works beyond the teaching environment. Yet, many parents are desperately seeking to get their children in full-time schools, supposing this teaching environment, who tends to keep their students for at least 7 hours in school, could be enough to grant a good-enough level of learning to get into a good university. However, the most important in the educational process is not the time invested in study, but the quality of the knowledge offered by the institution. As such, in Amazonas, few full-time schools tops the ranking of more vestibular approvals on the most renowned public universities.

The educational process is a social process in its uttermost concept, and must have an active participation of everyone interested in its building; Governments, society, and especially active participation of the students' families in basic education. Certainly, the more well groomed students are those whose parents directly follow their everyday learning, aiding with both homework and discipline.

The weight that formal education, adequate use of computational systems and technical knowledge hold in modern society is enough reason to have families playing a larger role in their children's education. By itself, it reinforces the need of parents in poorer families, aided by school's supervising systems, attempt to legate to their children a higher level of proper education as means to leave poverty, especially as the other alternative would have been the crime.

Reconstructing the public national educational system will need hundreds of thousands of urgent improvements, beginning with the efforts of governments and teachers in a higher quality management, families' commitment to their children's learning and, unavoidably, the injection of much more financial resources to increase the average of investment per student, which is still too low in comparison with other countries with better public school systems.

Nonetheless, the initial efforts for the transformation of a bankrupt public system into a dynamic, modern and at least less inefficient model, besides being more adapted to the mentality and aptitudes of the youth nowadays, can be focused in four topics of intervention, applied ever since the early years of school:

- Improvements in teachers' intellectual needs;
- Adaptation of the scholar curriculum to a post-modern age;
- Building lighter, modern physical spaces;
- Introduction of mobile teaching tools.

Statistics show, and test results do not deny, that the basic formation of the teachers in the worst schools is far from adequate, and most do not perform in their specific field. In other words, the schools are taking any professionals, regardless if they are apt to compose their rankings, without care for the negatives and distortions of this arrangement. On the other hand, for the public school to attract better qualified professionals, it is necessary to have a better financial compensation as in any market, as in sports, where high-roller clubs pay the best salaries to players who can achieve more titles. Still, by paying better salaries and demanding exclusiveness from the teachers, it is possible to adequate their labor hours into preparation, teaching a continuing in after class systems. In other words, it is necessary to keep the teachers for at least seven daily hours in school, giving time to compose and prepare courses and still being available to after class programs, including the possibility of remote courses.

Brazilian scholar curriculum is deeply late, and the students perceived this fact long time ago. A modern curriculum would be introduced through a system that covers all the essential, obligatory subjects and includes optative subjects, always backed up by fundamental requirements, among which participation in community voluntary work, project development in NGOs or philanthropic institutions, valuing the participation of the students in organizations who perform works tied to the awareness of citizenship and solidarity.

A modern curriculum must also obligatorily present online classes, inside or outside school, which would allow the students to access, assimilate and build abstract models of learning organization through remote systems. By doing so, contents like the Punic Wars would seem so fresh that the students would be amazed and hooked up until the last chapter of Carthage's destruction, in a way to relate with mercantilism, colonialism and European wars fought in search of an ultramarine market, for instance.

The school is, above all, a collective of knowledge aimed at reproducing and producing more knowledge, since childhood making individuals learn the main principles that condition life in society and culture. Long ago, when time and space where absolute and inseparable from the context of daily life, all the content necessary to the learning process were restricted to the places of teaching, like public libraries, or in the printed books someone could buy. Nowadays, where time and space are relative, knowledge and information are found scattered across thousands of servers and informatics' centers, and are able to be browsed from everywhere in the world. Thus, school as a physical space tends to lose importance in this process, who needs to be operated by offering extra contents to thousands of students in closed interactive networks such as Facebook or Instagram, as a way of reinforcing traditional knowledge with modern tools widely used by the teenagers and young people, and in the future will serve as an essential tool in both work and process of learning.

It is even worth mentioning that the deeply mobile nature of work, leisure and knowledge in modern days allows the construction a mobile, innovative pedagogy, named "learning mobile". It reinforces even further that a physical place named school one day shall disappear as central, focused structure of learning, and can someday be constituted essentially of learning networks where students may hang around multiple rooms with different contents of teaching, in countless networks of knowledge and information, just like affinity groups are formed online. Yet, while this futurist model is not materialized, it should at least begin with multiple subjects' tools, whose presented content is available in remote interactive networks, coordinate by teachers and a pedagogical body responsible for its maintenance and revision.

I worked in a school where there was a modern informatics lab, but nobody used it. I questioned the school's board why, and the answer was that it was necessary to present a pedagogical project to use it. As I really wanted to open the school to that modern world's preciosity, I presented two projects; one quite generalist, and the other for digital education for seniors.

Many teachers were impressed seeing me teaching in a modern informatics lab, and so were the 38 other classes who were excluded from its utilization. However, what startled me the most was the fact that the lab was already set up for at least two years, and nobody had the wise idea of using it as a pedagogical resource for enhancing the performance of the students.

My happiness was to verify that those simple classes allowed the first contact of many people with a modern computer, whose creation in this form was at least 30 years old and, by the lack of availability of a schemed system of learning achieved a status of advanced technology exclusion, where the simpler operations in a PC became a truly incomprehensible mathematical sentence.

In modern societies, the rate of progressive, safe growth begins with the strengthening of systems of creation and transmission of knowledge, especially in a world where the economic value of knowledge has become central and highly differential, and its availability constitutes the greatest resource of strategic competitiveness for the cities who wish to attract investors and relevant companies, and for the people who effectively want to work in said companies. The transformation of an industrial, violated and late society into a healthy, technical and comfortable society. It must the focus of families, companies and people who intend to achieve a better position in the social structures of the world, who is quickly consolidating as post-modern, post-industrial and post-patriarchal.

Certainly, the construction of a society whose knowledge is a differential factor, necessarily preceding reforms on its late structures, which linger in our country and in the mentality of its inhabitants, as the lack of environmental awareness, lack of sense of collective citizenship, lack of respect for the indigenous and African traditions. Especially, in the lack of offering a public structure of essential services, aiding and producing a sense of comfort and mutual security to all of its citizens, and so allowing the cities to exist as a reference for the attraction of productive long-term investments and skilled professionals for academic extension.

As such, while society does not understand that the educational process is long and difficult and requires mutual sacrifices between teachers, governments, parents and students, the country will remain in its average issuing students without basic knowledge of their mother tongue nor math, and professionals without the adequate qualifications to face the challenges of the modern age. As a result, it would allow the construction of aware citizens, groomed to occupy essential posts for the State's government, which is the main point of a country must aim to be developed, fair and prosperous.

References Chapter III

1. IBGE – Brazilian Statistic Yearbook 1936
2. Anuário Estatístico Brasileiro 1950
3. BEISEGEL, Celso de Rui, **Estado e educação popular: um estudo sobre a educação de adultos.**
4. IBGE – Brazilian Statistic Yearbook 1995
5. José Eustáquio Romão, Ivanise Monfredini, **Prometeu Desencantado**, pp. 50, 51.
6. IBGE, National Research per House, 2014
7. Ibidem
8. Superior Education Chart in Brazil 2015– SEMESP
9. Ibidem
10. Ibidem
11. Brasil - Country Note - Education at a Glance 2015: OECD Indicators,
12. DataPopular Institute, 2012
13. Ibidem
14. exame.abril.com.br/economia – 07-02-2017
15. g1.globo.com/economia/noticia/2015/09/ - 22-01-2017
16. Joseph E. Stiglitz, **Making Globalisation Work**, 2006,
17. Brasil - Country Note - Education at a Glance 2015: OECD Indicators,
18. www.oecd.org/pisa/keyfindings/pisa-2015-results-overview.pdf
19. Nonaka & Takeuchi, **On Knowledge Management**, 2008
20. Ibidem
21. Ibidem
22. Joseph E. Stiglitz, **Making Globalisation Work**, 2006.

> The times are liquid because, like water, it changes quickly. In contemporary society, nothing is made to last.
> Zygmunt Bauman

IV – Jobs and Careers

Last decades produced a hurricane of new ideas, new behaviors and new attitudes, and a large array of management tools and interaction process, which deeply transformed all of our lives and helped remodel the more relevant traits of society, after the wide scale introduction of new computational technologies. The feeling these technological advancements cannot offer comfortable boundaries fall short on logic, helping to sow an uncomfortable social position between families, people, social relations and specially the possibility of building a solid professional career, in a world tending to absolutely discard the stability and long-term contracts.

In this world, thousands of professionals are suffering suffocating pressures by the ever-growing introduction of technologies who automatize process, generate value, change flows and aid management, letting go on people who are not productive enough in their jobs in every economic sector. In this highly exclusive environment, we are all pressure every day for reinvention of ourselves, aiming to acquire new skills and abilities to become relevant for the maintenance of the careers that remain important to governments and enterprises.

The Difficult Art of Valuing Talents

The search for talents became a highly relevant issue for most organizations. However, many of said organizations who feel the necessity to hire talents do not perceive they do not have to look out, because they are already among their ranks. They only need to be perceived, challenged, conducted and valued, in order to give back to the company in exchange for the trust earned.

As hard as it may seem, intellectual capital, so prized by the market, is often available, underrated and unappreciated in many companies whose managers cannot comprehend the organizational reality in its total, letting go of the company people who would soon be a huge asset to another company.

Long time ago, I worked in an enterprise in Manaus's Industrial Park, issuing administrative services. The company was small, and its only organized departments were the fiscal, importation of materials and payment, while the other departments were organized according to the urgent needs.

In a certain occasion, I was responsible for the buys of a few goods needed in administration support services. Thus, I started organizing the larger buys and directed them to wholesaling companies. After a dozen buys, my manager perceived I was saving around 60% of the costs, and asked me to perform the same job in the acquisition of raw material. After new buyouts, she perceived the same efficiency in cutting the companies expenses. So, she made a tempting offer: she proposed that I changed my job, assuming the head of the buyouts and the stock, and said that I should be content for being recognized as a competent guy, who would be soon be receiving a raise salary. I went home so happy, thinking about getting married soon, because in only eight months of company I would be promoted already. The sky was only the beginning of the limit.

After a few weeks building what did not existed in an organized manner in that enterprise, and she informed me that, in order to give my dreamed raise she only needed the authorization of the director, who would be in town briefly and wanted to chat with me face to face. When the day came, the director came to the company and invited me to a meeting. I was really excited, for he was known for his reserved character and avoided taking to employees of posts beneath manager.

He began the meeting in the skin of the Italian explorer Marco Polo, famous for his explorations of Asia a long time ago, by telling me about his travels to Europe, China, Hong Kong and the Moon, for all that mattered, and remarked how hot my town is – something we, amazonenses, could not perceive ourselves. By listening to those fantastic stories, I could tell that there was not going to be a raise, because any competent manager would start the meeting by thanking my dedication and work for granting the efficiency in the company's more needed aspect: its costs. By listening only tales of far away lands, I started to realize that he wanted to tell me that only when I could travel the world, I would be worthy of recognition and a proper raise, although at the time we were 40 years apart, and it would take a long time.

Considering that I did not wanted to wait that long to have the financial recognition for my ability of working efficiently I decided to leave the company, and by doing so, I had to listen to a passionate speech about how unfair I was being, because for many, injustice and ingratitude is always the others. Unfortunately, it is still a latent reality, especially in a country where people are classified and hierarchized based on their place of birth, putting decaying hyenas in charge of lions, because the latter were not born in the symbolic savannah of the douchebag imagination of those bad managers.

Remembering this anecdote few months ago, while passing by that company, I had the first motivation to write this book, in order to share with people who in spite of their hard work cannot be valued or recognized as talents and assets, who, unlike me gave up on trying to invest on themselves and ended up accepting their superiors' stupidity as determining and impossible to overcome.

My answer is clear: keep investing in yourself, because knowledge is power and as the time goes by, those who know more and seek to reinvent and readapt themselves to new realities are always those who remain standing, confident that everything can be improved and amplified. These are the people who torn the corporate world less dull and lost in a robot-like process.

I worked in another company where promotions and recognition were determined by time of service in the company, thus leaving many of the employees working with nothing but one motivation: waiting for the time to pass and the promotions to arrive. I was always a critic of this system, especially because the promotions were achieved only after 7 or 8 years of work, and I, 23-years old at the time, was already married and needed to make more money to provide tranquility and comfort to my family.

By the way, when I decided to marry so young, many friends and coworkers asserted it was more important, even mandatory, to make more money, get more mature and more stable in a career and after all those "more", I would be fit to marriage. At the time I taught math and responded, honestly, that considering the properties of the science, the order of the operands does not change the result. As of, as I trusted myself, I could marry first and then get mature, and then make money, and finally getting old, without altering the result of the José Walmir person. So, as a result of the multiplication is the same independent of the order of the operands, I married, and remain married until today thanks to my wife's patience.

In the company where the employees had to get old to be promoted, I started to work as if already a manager, which was the first relevant promotion. After a year of hard work, I was indeed promoted to manager, earning the distrust of many other employees. Nonetheless, thanks to my dedication, I was a great manager, earning a few prizes like perks and travels.

Many colleagues admired my work and asked what I did in order to be promoted to manager so soon, to which I replied: work, study and think like a manager, because when you get promoted, nothing will be new - except for the raise. The rest will be already your routine.

Back then, I worked in a private-sector enterprise and taught math in a public school. In a teacher meeting, many coworkers briefed me, beforehand, that there was a tough class, and that I should join the other teachers in trying to fail as many students as I could. I was deeply shocked perceiving that the class they were trying to sabotage was my favorite class, which I considered the more skilled in school.

In my analysis, the restraint a few teachers tried to impose at the class was due to the students higher capacity of arguing, seen that many teachers and a handful of other narcissistic professionals hate to be questioned, confronted or less informed than their subordinates. There are many ways to achieve a common goal, and their method was to try to sever the modernizing impulse that proposes itself to do so.

And so life goes on. In every institution, organization and space, there are still professionals who out of fear, insecurity, envy or narcissism, chose to deny the value of changing and innovation, and by doing so they compromise the result and efficiency of the organization and, in a few cases, tent to compromise the very existence of the others, by denying their values.

I always believed in myself and in my abilities, and always invested so that I would not be just one man without purpose trying to change the world, because I know the world will change with or without me. Independent of what the citizens-of-the-world "managers" understood about people, I always tried to do the best in the organizations I worked, until it was time to say goodbye. I always believed that any professional should constantly have in mind the necessity to study, work, readapt and share knowledge, aiming to not because nor prisoner nor hostage of the incompetent hyenas that rule many organizations nowadays, in order to decide for yourself how, when and with whom you intend to live and work. Thus, like Diogenes replied to the great Alexander when asked what he wanted, you can someday say to the hyenas: stand out of my sunlight... and hasta la vista, baby.

The Bad Heritage of the Military Corporation

Many of the organizational practices existing nowadays were built in a time and space far away from ours, by people who read reality in a complete different manner, introducing the limited reading content they had in the management practices and process of their time. A few of those practices became completely outdated, others are questionable and should never be put into action, given that many traits of the main form of thinking and managing at the time produced a limited, ancient vision of work, which still echoes constantly in modern management by professionals who consider discipline and submission more important that responsibility and creativity.

The slaving past of our country produced a huge distortion on how institutions are organized, or personal relations and especially on how people perceive social and economic differences. The inhuman conditions of exploitation of labor work, which lasted centuries, left deep marks in modern society, especially on how we perceive criminality and job opportunities.

In the beginning of the last century, the country had little more than three thousand enterprises spread across several states, being that only after the deflagration of the World War I and the ferocious crises on the coffee price is when the industrial sector began to gain economic and political relevance. In the 1930's, after the fall of the old oligarchic republic and the beginning of the country's industrialization during the Vargas' government, most of the population lived on the countryside, completely marginal to the public systems of health, education and social security. In the cities, the few technical courses were reserved to the sons of elite and colonels, while most of the population barely had a primary level education, and few saw the pursuit of formal education as means to leave poverty and the toughness of the field labor. In the countryside, it was always needed more arms willing to work hard than brains willing to think. Thanks to the high rate of people residing in the countryside, aligned with the difficulties in maintenance of schools and the lack of interest of the elites in promoting access to universal education, we had in 1950 a rate of 50% of illiterate population in 1950, being the population of 15 years old or older being completely illiterate by the time's standards.[1]

Brazil at the time entered the age of industrialization with a huge chunk of its population as illiterates, a central structure of power in the hands of a dictator and pressured by the military, which more and more deflected firm their occupations as an army, dedication more time to the "government affairs", serving and interfering with public administration services and trying to somehow condition the administrative management of the enterprises, which should be seen as a disciplinary managements instead of pursuing the professional qualification of its managers and collaborators.

In 1920, only 20% of the Brazilian population lived in urban areas. By the decade of 1950[2], this number reached 50%, and the public teaching system, along other government enterprises, did not caught up with the population's growth spur, had no intention of creating professional courses or perfecting the already existing labor force, despite the necessity of increasing production. This necessity grew mainly because of the physical expansion of factories and incorporation of new workers to the industrial process through a system known as intensive work production systems, as an overcompensation to the lack of intellectual capital and the lack of advanced machinery and tools that could enhance productivity. Yet, in many cases, the production expanded by the simply importing productive blueprints from anywhere else in the world, which utilized less people as labor force, but with a higher specialization level.

The process of governmental incentives to the massive industrial production began in the 1930 and defined the form of spatial occupation of the modern cities, as would condition the population concentration in places where the factories settled, especially in areas near the political power who held most of the wealth. These places grew as result of directing public money to productive incentives instead of investing in education and infrastructure, given that the *fast industrialization had not only economic, but political and social effects. The factories have a privileged position in the cities, and as such, the Vargas Era is associated with a period of intense urbanization.*[3]

74

The so-called National Enterprise, stimulated by the State and protected of the imported goods' competition, was organized similarly to a military squadron of the time, as the administrative manager represented the Colonel, with a handful of technicians to coordinate the productive chain as Lieutenants which demanded order and discipline from a huge quantity of Foot Soldiers, the basic workers. These workers usually had no formal education whatsoever, and were introduced in this gigantic mechanical process of repetitive, timed tasks, supervised and dictated by the new labour laws edited by the central government, as the *direct intervention of the State in economy and in the work relations resulted directly of the late stage of Brazilian capitalism.*[4]

This combination of military-like enterprises, illiteracy, a population scattered all over the country, weak public investments in education and national market almost closed to the importation of many products made very difficult and distant the possibility of investments, public or private, directed at the necessity of educating the labor force. This fed in the tip of the productive chain the low quality of the products and services offered, primitive in comparison to the same products produced on other countries, aligned with the absence of a national company who offered durable goods, as this *industry demands capital volume, advanced technology, specialized labor and managing skills*[5], and all those items were rare on the country at the time.

This military enterprise worked properly at the time, because the intensive use of labor force required more strength and discipline than technical differentials. It demanded feeble flux of information among the managers, few, simple analysis, almost no technological or administrative innovations, and the incentives to the collaborators were usually violent and disciplinary in nature.

Still, conditioned by how society perceived families, religion and government, it was sought to gather all masculine, homogenous groups, seeking to mitigate the difficulties of adaptation to the factory's work, soften the structure of power division and discourage the process of innovation, empowered by the difficulties in changing the ranks of workers.

Another negative point, important for this type of organization, is that not promoting any form of intellectual stimulation inside the company, and limiting the possibility of developing particular skills, it would keep its employees apathetic, impeded of searching more efficient forms of self-improvement, both personal and financially. In a market who does not demand any specific qualification, both labor force and mechanical pieces could easily be replaced when they no longer fit in the industrial process.

The development of this national, military enterprise, was propelled by the governmental strategy and stapled through the well know model of substituting importations, trying to produce within the nation goods who were imported before. However, the government only encouraged the production of final goods, without concerning for the production of capital goods (industrial machinery, for instance), especially because the production of such goods require a high level of technical knowledge, high investments in education and qualification of personnel and the creation of structures aimed at such goal.

Even though the national enterprise was a deficient operational structure, the process of late industrialization made possible for the economy to grow at a rate of 7% among the final years of the World War II and the beginning of the decade of 1980[6]. Even though the country was operated by a semiliterate labor force, managed by inflexible administrators without qualifications and ruled by a government more concerned about an allegedly threat to homeland security than with the construction of an efficient educational system. This deficit constructed a wealthy nation, but deeply unequal, with few improvements and without investments on the education of promising employees.

In the same period, while Brazil lived the growth of base Industries mechanically organized under a semi military rule, strictly hierarchized and composed basically by people who could not read, geniuses like Dave Packard and Robert Noyce took the modern management culture to a whole new level, when *the management hierarchy was flattened (...) to create a culture that included Friday beer bashes, flexible hours and stock options*[7].

The technological and management delay who lingered for an above acceptable time in our country became more perceivable after the decade of 1980, when the model of industrial growth used until then, via substituting importations, ran dry. At the time, the GDP of Brazil grew only 1,5% per year, instituting an economic and social chaos face the urgent necessity of modernizing the industrial park and the difficulty of creating new jobs for the generation born after the military coup, in 1964, for a nation who became essentially urban, full of inequalities and urgent social demands.

The changes in technological, operational and management bases happening elsewhere in the world gave clear signs of the rising of other types of business structures, less bound to specific process and mechanical gears tightly connected, but more agile and flexible, more creative and dynamical, dismissing the excessive brutalities of the last system of administration.

Unfortunately, this sort of innovative structure did not immediately rose in Brazil, especially considering that the government was a centralizing dictatorship. Besides that, the State held grasp of the economy through investment banks, credit control, monetary exchange, and administration of inefficient public enterprises, badly managed by people who had ties to the power.

Any economic growth process with purely industrial basis must be necessarily followed by the renovation and continuous improvement of the technological means of production, as management and process systems. It would require a high level of financial and intellectual capital, in a dialectical process where the new technologies will start to require new skills, which can only me achieve through an educational system that values research and extension on knowledges.

Besides, there were still countless other structural difficulties which limited the transformation of a late industrial economy into a modern, dynamic one. First, the low on the internal resources limited the capacity of investing in capital goods with the country's own assets beyond the already existing expense on research and innovation. In addition, the patronage of the public bank's endeavors considered that the resources to found projects were more of a question of who would be the receivers, instead of thinking on the purpose, occasioning in absurd damage to banks in federal and regional banks, and he banks of investment cumulated immense debt and profited almost nothing, with few cases of success.

The formation of intellectual capital and its funding to turn abstract ideas into concrete solutions needs an elevated investment in education, in scientific research and extension, neglected by both the government and the national, retarded elites, who always saw education as enemy to their status quo. In a country were rarely a Guilherme Guinle shows up to do things differently every generation, the abyss between the level of knowledge existing in the world and the amount of knowledge Brazilian people can afford grows even larger, delaying and limiting the possibilities of approaching Brazilian technological industry to the best organizational practices around the world. So, the educational delay is still one of the biggest damages our country needs to face nowadays, and one of the main obstacles for the social and political development. The application of knowledge in the industrial production system has been a determining factor on economic and social growth in the last decades and the main actor in changing resources to concrete solutions to his citizens and enterprises' problems.

One of the great lessons history has taught us is that it is impossible to regain the time lost, and much harder to reorganize a wrecked social and economic system, built ineffectively, composed by ill-educated managers and a labor force with almost no education, with huge difficulties to get properly reeducated. This helped to cement the idea that the only organizational condition proper to the feebly educated workers was the imposition of unconditional order and discipline without questions, similar to the slaves in the 19th century's farms and the military quarters in the 20th century, where blacks and soldiers were nothing but pawns in a chess game. Unfortunately, this military enterprise, disciplined and brutally hierarchized left its prints in how we conceive work and many unprepared managers still look up to it as a reference.

Nowadays, both the armies and the enterprises need less a huge amount of unqualified personnel, especially for operational and daily activities, and more people with baggage, formal knowledge, skills in interacting with computational systems, and able to create a healthy relationship with the work environment, given that the main resources whose possession and management provides the primary source of wealth and power are nowadays, in the postindustrial era, knowledge, inventiveness, imagination, the ability to think and the courage to think differently[8].

Management, Intellectual Capital and Entrepreneurial Survival

Every research points the Brazilian people as one of the most prone to business endeavors in the world, be it for the total of formal enterprises open every year, be it for the simple desire to own a business when there is a possibility, be it through the scattered informal business. Nonetheless, the goal of being an entrepreneur goes against countless situations and circumstantial difficulties, especially for the small entrepreneurs, with low capital resources and a business restricted to its own small environment, making that in Brazil, for every 10 companies born, 6 will close the doors within five years, reaping dreams, resources and employs.

According to a recent data study, from the 694,5 thousand companies founded in 2009, only 275 thousand, or around 39%, were still working in 2014[9]. After the first year of activity, almost 23% of said companies shut down. This clearly indicates the difficulties of maintaining a profitable business, even if it is informal, can be higher than most new entrepreneurs imagine when defining their business plans, and without necessary organization, and a level of management accordingly to the fundamental traits evert activity demands, it is hard to survive for so long in markets that grow more competitive every day.

If we ask the owners of the companies who could not make it past the first five years what were the reasons of the premature fall of their business, certainly many would argue that the main reason was the excessive tributary loads and the overwhelming government's bureaucracy who difficult and inhibits the growth of new business. But if we analyze closely the main reason of the early death of those companies, we could more properly argue that the main deficiency is in the quality of the management and poor organizational practices given by this managers, for one simple reason. The Government works equally badly for every company, while the administrative question is individual, particular to the owner and manager of a business. If the main reason were the weight of taxes or bureaucracy, every company born in the same period would go bankrupt together, and those who survive would be working in a fraud scheme, irregularly, evading taxes or hiring workers without proper remuneration, which cannot be happening to most companies.

The same research points out that Amazonas registered the second lowest rate of survival for new enterprises, only behind Amapá, which means our state is the vice-leader on bankruptcy of business ventures. This numbers reflect in a general difficulty for all sectors and levels of the economy, confirming that the greatest difference between the surviving and the dying companies is the quality of management, that should be more focused on develop and apply knowledge in the operation process through continuous innovation than the sheer will of the owner to become an entrepreneur.

Another great difficulty many companies face is the lack of comprehension that many consumers of the modern age acquired a high level of information about products and services, called *prosumer*, making almost impossible to remain in the market without investing on the necessary "updates" their clients continuously desire, or without offering products and services according to the standards they seek. These companies nourish expectations that the price can be the only differential, without realizing that the consumers rely on information when buying, and are strongly influenced by the technological utilization than any other factor, including price.

Thus, to reach a comfortable position regarding the aimed business and conduct it for a long time, it is important to recognize that:

- Knowledge is a trully diffential fator in the quality of the business;
- The market is and always will be intensely competitive;
- Modern consumers are well informed; and
- Management is the more advanced factor in business competitiveness.

Sheer entrepreneur's excitement and availability of the necessary resources in an economic endeavor are not enough to remain in a profitable and safe all along the way, and without an exact notion of how complex the operational and management operations require, many of these companies begin already in retard. Their managers cannot produce enough knowledge to keep up with the changes and adaptations the external market requires, or at the same pace their competitors are searching, making frail and repetitive practices inefficient and inaccurate to the application in business, nowadays conduct in a complete different manner, where:

> Only a few companies have shown the capacity of changing so fast (...) and deal with the complexities involved. One of the main reasons why companies fail is the tendency to eliminate paradoxes, clinging to old routines created by their last success.[10]

In Amazonas, thanks the Industrial Park, the great business groups of external capital bring along their productive structures, means of work and management technics from other parts of the world, the majority of the managers, specialist in risk analysis and intern hearing, leaving few posts of high administration to the amazonenses. However, in the local companies there is a lack of qualified staff to compose the strategic board of administration, largely because their traditional education is flawed and limited, creating a relatively concerning scenario, both for the Manaus Industrial Park, for not finding certain professionals, and for the Manaus' people themselves, who start to see the foreigners as a threat.

Another relevant question that largely affects the life of new business is the unfamiliarity with the market they intend to conquer, making many of this companies simple ventures, without experience nor organization enough to remain alive, where a few will thrive as the others will not because in the market there are no blank spaces. Or the company grows and establishes, or other companies will do it in its stead, shamelessly.

A research performed by SEBRAE[11] in 2013 about survival of companies discovered that the sectors of civil construction and services are the most troubled in their first years, and from the total amount of companies founded in 2007 and 2010, approximately 72% in Brazil, while 56% and 58% in Brazil, shut down in up to five years. In Amazon, almost half the companies of services and civil construction could not survive this period, seen that for the companies open in 2007, the rate of survival was of 62% for industry, 66% for commerce and 49% for services[12]. The second worst data of the region, ahead only of Acre, a state with a much less dynamic and more traditional economy.

This indicators are deeply concerning for all the population, because the service's sector is the more dynamic in the modern economy, and the one of who goes through most reshaping. According the Annual Service Research – PAS – of the IBGE, in 2014 there were a million of non-financial enterprises, profiting around 1,4 trillion reais and employing around 13 million people[13]. Considering that this sector is the most dynamic of the post-modern world and tends to be more and more specific, the closing of so many companies clearly indicates a necessity in improving the enterprises' administration, which can allow many newborn companies to have competitiveness conditions to keep themselves longer and more professionally in the market.

Service's sector has presented a larger deficit in attracting better-graduated professionals onto their ranks. Although it is not possible to assert with accuracy if there is a direct relation between the survival rate of an enterprise and the scholarship of the owner/manager, it is likely that the most vulnerable enterprises are those who show limited capacities on technological innovation and on investment in intellectual capital, the cornerstones of any enterprise aimed at providing services or corporative support. The composition of capital becomes more and more important in the business world, and directly relates to the amount of necessary investment for the implantation and operation of a company, especially the intellectual capital it can apply in its structures, which is one of the major factors on the survival and balance of an enterprise.

The composition of the necessary capital needed to raise a business can be both financial (money, machinery and equipment) and intellectual, for differential utilization in new business niches. The statistics show that the higher the amount of investment in the construction of a new business, the higher the chance it can remain operating for the first five years. Be it by the financial sum invested in its foundation, which cold difficult the settling of new competitors, be it by the specificity of the intellectual capital used, which requires years of construction, practice and in hard times, it is the latter what will allow the search for new solutions that will help to keep the company alive and steady.

Financial capital in new business is usually property of the companies' owners, for there are technical limitations when it comes to financing newborn companies, and it is often a bad idea to start and endeavor in debt. However, companies founded upon the bases of intellectual capital usually uses the financial founds of the third party which precisely makes it run properly, especially in sectors like informatics and technology, where an idea comes from one bright mind and founded by another mind who intends to profit from the former's idea. In this aspect, companies on the Age of Knowledge are the most sought after for financing from third parties in a global scale, for they essentially work with information and networks and seek to offer services differently from their competitors, cleaner, cheaper and more functional, or simply seek to aid the preexisting systems in a safer way.

For such innovator enterprises, James Collins and Jerry Porras, in their oeuvre "Built to Last" forged the term "the genius of the AND" to describe the companies who became more dynamic and successful and perceived better the changes in modern markets. For the authors, these companies can sum paradoxes instead of limiting or dividing them, given that:

> Visionary companies do not brutalize themselves with the "Tyranny of the OR"—the purely rational view that says you can have either A OR B, but not both. They reject having to make a choice between stability OR progress; cult-like cultures OR individual autonomy; home-grown managers OR fundamental change; conservative practices OR Big Hairy Audacious Goals; making money OR living according to values and purpose. Instead, they embrace the
> "Genius of the AND"—the paradoxical view that allows them to pursue both A AND B at the same time.[14]

The illustration of the "genius of and" does not fit into the model of many outdated organizational structures of many companies, who traditionally founded their management and organizational activities upon the concept "or" – or we do is one way or another. It seeks to bring together every possibility to create a balanced operational flow, efficient and dynamic, and only after a juxtaposition of countless possibilities comes the effective appropriation of knowledge to make available the capacities and innovation that only few business manage to achieve.

The numbers presented show clearly that companies who survive and thrive year after year are those who sunk in these new management skills necessary to shared work and those who built the minimum requirements to administrate and progress efficiently, in a constantly changing world that demands from new managers a much larger commitment with specific, continuous learning and professionalism. To keep bringing the company up to strategic positions, thinking about the business knowledge, client's anxiety, product's differential, competitors and the dynamics of a hard to define market, it is essential to have skill to read and understand its sigs even outside the conventional routes, unlike most companies. On the other hand, these complex situations started to present many possibilities of profit and success to those who can read in between the lines, who have more content and skills to offer and beyond their ability of management, can also assure the maintenance of the company's dreams and plans into a likely future.

Omniscient Generals-Managers ISO 9999

When I was in high school (secondary school), I was invite into a student's union whose goal was to promote different activities that could contribute with the quality of the learning and that could aid the interactions between the students and the teachers. After the team was complete, I resigned in advance of that important project, because in every meeting we had I asked the union's future director what were our main goals, to which he replied that they were all in his head, and once we were "entitled" we'd all see what HE would develop in the school, what HE had in mind.

This little anecdote clearly exemplifies situations that still happen often in the business environment, by administrators who consider that all the management necessary to the routine of work and organization is within their bright, omniscient and creative minds. These professionals thank for the contribution of their collaborators only when they serve the purpose of flattering them and confirming what they already think about themselves; that they know it all, and much more. Creative and inventive people know that the construction of knowledge begins by the certainty of the doubt and ignorance about countless subjects. Unfortunately, one of the most important conditions for the perpetuity of the mediocrity and lack of intelligence is precisely to assume to know a lot about many subjects, or to assume there is no more to learn.

The refined knowledge is a product of the certainty of ignorance, along the will to learn and the necessary resources to a continuous and disciplined learning.

Aligned with the lack of perception of their own ignorance, it is even possible to assert that many of the negative traits that limit the work of such managers were forged during most of the last century, when Brazil was administrated, in different degrees, by authoritarian governments, conservative and centralizing, that would dismiss the popular claim and the people's most urgent needs in the fashion of a slaver farm in the 19th century. These regimens punished with disproportional force those who demanded a better administrative posture, more democratic and less bureaucratic, and those who sought to create laws in order to protect the marginalized people.

The authoritarian political management, which went from violently imposing the president of the republic to the far boundaries of the colonel's domains, had (and still have) a strong influence on how Brazilian people administrate their families, courthouses, enterprises and many other public interest organizations. Even today, it is possible to find professionals whose management style prizes certain traits, like strict discipline, respect for fixed hours of work and unconditional respect to the hierarchy as if in a military facility, where the boss is a General, or even a Colonel of the old Amazon, daily concerned about war rituals and possible enemies to his *cosmopotroglodyte's* vision about management, ideals and people.

Alexander the Great, one of the greatest military generals in occident's history[15,] left his major legacy in transferring the effective political power of the world known as Asia Minor to the Western Europe, where the power remained until the conclusion of the World War II, although it still is a huge influence on the minds of military, artists, legislators and even admnistrators. Even though as a general he was ruthless, he was also intelligent, charismatic and had a particular vision on how to command his troops: never order anyone to do something he was not willing to do himself. To him, assuming necessary risks, weighting the orders, delegating tasks proportionally and motivating the troops was essential to the success of his conquests and consolidation of his power.

The ancient world was a ravaged by war for power, territory, women and money. The empires were not formed in a consensus but by the arbitrary imposition of military conquests, grating loot for the winners, moral obedience for the defeated, and taxes payment as a form of loyalty and warning to those who defied the imperial supremacy.

However, thousands of years after the premature death of Alexander the Great, many managers still believe that the market is a bloody battlefield and to win it is necessary to position their work strategies based in a destructive competition, mistakenly mirroring battles and military tactics, instead of managing based on ideals of cooperation and commitment. Not only being cooperative among the areas of the company, but also with the external collaborators and the social environment that keep the company alive, making sure that the professionals do not see their tasks as an imposition, but as simultaneously dependent on the other's tasks, materializing on the construction of one complex, more than just the sum of its parts. But it is not an easy task to realize, given that the notion of interdependence is rare to managers who cannot organize time, resources and people.

Long ago, I took a training for managers coordinated by instructors from the prestigious Getúlio Vargas Foundation (FGV), because of the low general capacity of the company's high-ranking managers. One of the first activities developed in this event was a dynamic aimed at analyzing the level of coordination and agility of people in a collective task, which started with the distribution of sheets labeled from 1 to 10 to each member of a group. Then, the instructor would say any number, and the objective was that each member rose the sheet with its respective number, and the final number would have to be the sum of the amount the instructor demanded, the fastest possible.

The first team executed the task, clumsily, in about 50 seconds. The instructor said the process could be improved and called the next group. The second team organized differently and managed to execute the task in around 30 seconds, almost half of the first. The third group managed it in about 15 seconds, an already great timing. After that, the instructor asked if anyone could do it faster.

To the astonishment of everyone, I raised my hand and said yes. That task could be done faster. Soon, the instructor asked me to show how, and the curious gathered around me.

First, I asked the last team to stand where they were and only the team "leader" to leave, changed some people's places, and waited for the initial order. After the instructor pronounced the number, we could manage the calculus in only six seconds. I believe it was some sort of record on that dynamics.

Everyone was impressed by our efficiency and asked how could be manage that time of execution, to which I replied: first, the team's greatest error was the fact that the "leader" raised his sheet first, remaining fairly comfortable when in comparison to his "followers", pushing on them the pressure, leaving them more concerned about missing the result than achieving the goal.

Second, it was perceivable that the members of the team came from a diverse academic background, and were badly displayed for the execution of the exercise, which went from a simple execution at first to a complex in the end, requiring that the last ones to raise the sheet to be more accurate and to pay more attention to the others.

At last, without any pressure to execute the task, the skills of everyone flowed smoothly, efficiently, as the pressure of the performance gave place to the factor "performance for result", and in no time everything was done properly and quickly.

Bringing this dynamic to our reality, it is possible to assert that it happens in many modern companies, where the bosses thinks of themselves as generals, and rest in comfortable positions as the only one who could possibly lead the troop, pushing goals, menacing and pressuring for results only the team. In fact, it should be the opposite. One of the noblest functions of a chief is to absorb, administrate and dissipate the everyday pressure of their collaborators, taking for himself or herself the decision of the toughest responsibilities, while directing people to their correct function, in time and without any sort of disrespect.

Outdated managers, like in the ancient myths, cult the figure of the ME, the leader in itself, the saint and lonely hero, who can alone solve the world's problems after what he understands as problems and their adequate solutions. These heroes communicate with others through riddles and pompous words, but nobody understand what they are supposed to mean. This character no longer finds support in modern companies, where the work mutually shared among collaborators and teams is much more valued than magical and miraculous solutions from lonely heroes who cannot communicate efficiently and cannot share their knowledge. The majority of the modern companies value much more sharing knowledge, experiences and proceedings, because they judge it the smarter way to keep steady efficiently on the long run, while lonely heroism is an isolate phenomenon, limited to a certain duration of time, resulting in positive results and fanatic supporters through the same mythical stories and Hollywoodian characters with no real connection to the real world.

Another concerning fact is how many managers delegate tasks to their professionals in an erroneous way, completely apart from their potential, in a permanent improvisation. Nowadays, most academic graduations serve to perform multiple functions and functional tasks in many areas of knowledge, as long as correctly managed inside the team. If a team is to homogenous it tends to be internally competitive, for the simple reason that, like simple organisms with little differentials, they tend to die more easily, for a simple problem can easily annihilate the group as a whole, while in heterogeneous groups it is easier to survive eventual attacks.

I always assert to my soccer friends that every manager want to have a team full of Messis and Iniestas and Cristiano Ronaldos, but nobody want to manage a Junior Baiano or a Barrote. The problem is that every team needs them both, and the error is to try to put a Messi to play in the defense and a Barrote on the attack. It will never work. But, when playing in different positions and with the right tools, both can be real stars. On the modern and competitive companies, one of the greatest advantages is on the fact that managers can extract the best of each individual and post them inside the teamwork, where they can be the more efficient possible, turning talents into results, results into innovations, and innovations into knowledge. Enterprises exist essentially to generate results: financial, social, patrimonial, cooperative, aggregating value to the brand, the stockers, collaborators and society as a whole.

Alexander the Great left a huge legacy in his time and beyond, serving as base to that ancient society, which little by little turns into a more complex one, where brute force, military discipline and the weight of the arms used to be of major importance for they allowed the fundamental conditions to running and imposing order and discipline in society whose main traits were the elitism, exclusive and slavery.

Thousands of years after Alexander's death, the modern optics value creative knowledge, shared work and participative collaboration to guide the thought of those who occupy management posts, whose main goal is to motivate people through professional commitment towards a common institutional goal. Be it producing goods and services, be it producing ideas to be applied on the improvements people and companies need, it must never forget that the world of ruthless generals and disciplined soldiers is over a long time ago and will not come back. To remain in this path is to remain alone when force and discipline fail, without responsibilities nor notion of sharing knowledge.

Companies Grow Up or Say Goodbye

Living, loving and working demands a conscious comprehension that people and companies are living beings who share mutual relations, facts and resources. This affirmation is more clearly perceivable when analyzing the route of companies who end their activities sadly, after glorious years of existence and affirmation of efficient productive model, offering differential products and services. Without a doubt that companies, like any living organism, are bound to born, grow, and transcend: beyond their existence, or into oblivion.

The beginning of the decade of 1980 was terrible for both enterprises and workers all over Brazil. The disastrous military government, censorship of statistic data and the second crash on oil's price in 1979 cause a huge public debt and diminished the liquid capacity of both public and private companies, resulting in an uncontrollable inflation and high levels of unemployment, misery and urban violence all over the country. It is still traumatic for a generation who lived with an economic growth rate of 8% with little real to no profit in life's quality. Besides, it was perceivable the lingering educational delay, followed by a technologically outdated industry, the high level of intervention on the economy by the government via its inefficient and badly managed public enterprises, maintained by political and familiar ties.

Most Brazilian companies at the time were composed by dying structures, operating and competing according to the model of protection of the national industry, based upon the import substitution models instead of the efficiency of goods and services offered to the internal market, unimpressed by the elevated prices and low-quality of products.

In an environment at the edge of the economic chaos, few managed to observe and absorb the peculiarities that shaped the most important traits in modern companies, governments and professions. Even fewer internalized the perception that organizations, much like people, are living beings, structured upon dependent interaction among their basic components.

Biological structures are constituted by thousands of cells united to play specific roles, constituting tissues and organs, totalizing larger structures, living beings, who interact with each other in an enormous chain of interaction and coexistence.

In this aspect, just like in living organisms, companies and institutions are also born, develop and, unless they are able to adapt, die. The scourge of business death is as cruel as the biological one, because it does not spare nor considers feelings, race, income, education or social position.

The notion that social systems, like enterprises, finds its support in the model of systemic conception of life. This system named Holism sees the world in mutual relations of cooperation and interaction, as integrated wholes, whose properties cannot be reduced to those of smarter unities[16]. It is inherent to the internal parts of the organism itself, external to the environment where its inserted and opposes strongly the mechanist, Cartesian traditional models.

Estranged from this vision and without fully understanding what the external environment will influence of the self-organization of the institution, many huge companies in the 1970's and 1980's did not manage to perceive the changes that took place in the work systems, and could not envision the whole paradigm taking shape with the introduction of computational systems. As a result, they were forced to adapt abruptly, without properly having time, and turned to the decade of 1990 already broken, acquired by other companies, or into intensive care waiting for a miraculous cure or a ruthless death.

Assuming we could watch the commercial ads of the 1980's, we would be impressed by how many companies had a fair share of space on prime time of Brazilian TV and suddenly disappeared, from the shelves and from the memories. Names like Varig, Vasp, Monark, Kolynos, Aripuanã, Bemiro, Marcly, Mesbla, Disco Laser, Atari, Bamerindus, National Bank, JVC, AIWA, BASF and Sharp are totally unrecognizable for people in their twenties. For those who became financially independent during the decade of 1980, these companies were symbols of ostentation and desire for many. Nonetheless, when the when the winds of change blew, many managers could not follow the fundamental essence of the new conditions which would soon become mandatory to the big companies. On that time, those companies were a reference in proving goods and services, and from that decade we, consumers, are left with nothing but sweet nostalgia, while the institutionalized managers remain bitter about how they could no longer fit on the market.

The lesson such organizations left to was is that companies are not beautiful, static monuments to be idolized by everyone; they are living beings, and they live with the goal to product something and thrive in a harsh environment. Like any other being, to keep existing healthily and actively, it must take an efficient position, seeking to eliminate the vices that would intoxicate its system, weakening it to death, and aiming at performing a function that will fill the necessities of the society.

Following this line of thought, Capra asserts that every living system, biological or social, are wholes whose specific structures result from the interdependence of its parts[17]. This would internally allow that the organism, internally, and the environment, externally, to interact simultaneously and mutually, interdependent between multiple components[18].

Therefore, most modern corporations are undeniably more organic than mechanic, geared up after mutual coexistence of countless processes and resources, including the human beings organized in sectors and larger, more decentralized departments, totalizing a unity aimed at interacting with the environment through a network of suppliers, collaborators investors and clients. This interaction between many components of the corporate organization mirrors the living things' system, the environment, which is the interaction between all physical, chemical, biological and social structures, gathered together and inseparable from the Earth.

To many professionals, the idea that enterprises are living organisms seems hard to assimilate, maybe because of the lack of knowledge about the functioning of the macro and micro universe, or the limits of their technical education. Nonetheless, just like the human body is a unique total of smaller components, the totality of people inserted in a larger collective environment, like a factory or a family, along other biological microsystems, sums up to make the whole ecosystem of our planet, a living structure sustained by the interactions of lesser subsystems. And as our planet is only a tiny component in an immense universe, we must recognize that, we are not only in the universe, but a part of it, so the universe itself is a living being just like us.[19]

There are some important traits shared among all living things, and, according to the systemic vision, are applicable to any modern institution, through self-knowledge about why to exist in an environment (which is the function an organism performs in it), being directly related to the capacity of internal organization and said organisms, independent from their external structures, continuously interacting with the renewal capacities of their multiple internal compounds which allows them to adapt.

Obviously, any organism, citizen or company develops a mechanism of internal organization of their compounds, which must be accordingly to the traits of their existence in the world. It fits the concept of value chain that any being builds or intend to develop during its existence. Self-organization binds molecules and chemical elements, cells to biological process, people to processes to companies and their distribution chain, in a way that the whole is the result of every individual process performed according to a plan previously structured. Conscious, mechanical, random or inducted by an external agent, it coordinates the process according to the needs of the larger organism.

In the living organisms, the influence of the external environment is reflected on the internal organization of the organism, seen that it is always the latter that controls its particular form of organization, adapting to the conditions imposed by the environment, instead the mean determining how the organism will behave. This relationships are usually mutually interdependent, instead of violently imposed.

Another important trait of the living beings is their capacity of self-renovation, which is nothing more than an effective mean of getting rid of old, battered compounds, damaged by lack of use or violence, or who simply lost their ability to work as a whole, determining even the human's life, which must end someday. As any other living structure, it comes a time when our bodies cannot fulfill its role, the natural progressive process of decay of our body and mind takes place, and then we are shut down completely. After that, we have another essential function: to serve as fertilizer so that other organisms can develop taking advantage of this process.

Without a doubt companies are living, productive structures, which seek to execute specific functions through the continuous interaction between the internal and external compound of the environment they are inserted in. The main factor to the its continuous operation is the ability to pave the conditions to remain alive, adapting and evolving with constant innovation, which is intrinsically bound to life, and allows every organism to remain preserved efficiently in its achievable future, independent of the role it performs.

We are the companies' health, efficiency, consciousness and happiness, and especially, its potential survival on the long run depends on how we live in it, conscious of a much bigger picture where we play a role. It intends to exist independent of our will, but it works only when understood in its more relevant traits.

Many times we believe that the company's problems are always the others, and lose great opportunities to build efficient solutions, not realizing that the others are also solutions. If we analyze deeply many of the enterprise's internal problems, certainly the lack of understanding about the function of other people and the difficulty to see it as a living structure who relates and shares, interdependent to other people and processes are major factors. It can be corrected only by sharing more than goals, knowledges and attitudes, by realizing that like most living beings, humans are whole interactions of countless flows and specific processes between millions of smaller unities, and whether we want it or not, work non-stop to proportionate us a healthy body and mind. We are existing in the same planet, inserted in a larger universe, composed by other stars and space energies, inseparable parts of a whole process of universal shared existence, like on R.E.M's song "You Are the Everything":

> The stars are the greatest thing you've ever seen
> And they're there for you
> For you alone, you are the everything

Because we are, like stars, products of the same matter, share the same origin and are bound to the same rules that condition life.

Why Work and to Whom?

Modern companies are living integrated organisms in a larger social and economic environment, whose main goal is to establish a work method that will allow it to carry on its business. By knowing how an organism shares, interacts with the environments and absorbs information, the organizations build the operational structure they judge necessary, whose main goal is to find adequate solutions to people's problems by providing services and goods and as a result increasing the brand's net worth, profiting and granting financial feedback to the investors and stock holders. Summing up, the goal is to help building a world where people feel fulfilled through hard work and inclusion.

There are many methodological, legal and sociological considerations about what can be done regarding the operational dynamics of any organization, capitalist or not. Bu one of the main conditions common to any organization who aims to be useful to life in society is the clear comprehension of the reason why any being exists.

The understanding of a corporate and institutional "me" is the nothing but the shared comprehension of oneself in the world and the reasons why act upon it as an institutions composed by countless different people, machinery, tools and processes to effectuate strategies.

This organizational "me", like the personal "me", is the particular form of acting and thinking in any organization, and must impose itself upon the collaborators as the main factor of collective participation on the daily actions, so that the company can concrete the goals it sought to build, being understood as:

> A collective sense of identity and fundamental finality. It is the organizational of the self-knowledge – the shared comprehension of what the company stands for, where it is going, and what type of world it intends to live, and what is more important, how to make this world a reality.[20]

To many professionals and companies, according to Nonaka and Takeuchi, the hardest question to answer is how to make a reality out of this intended world. Seen that the business environment became deeply competitive, the consumers became more demanding and the great certainty in the post-industrial world is the uncertainty of the next day. In this ocean of uncertainty, knowledge becomes a differential tool and a highly differential factor of competitiveness to the companies and professionals who can produce it and adjust it to their daily demands as the main factor to construct efficient and healthy processes and safer work structures. This method will put the company steadily ahead of its competitors, is determining to the process of creative offering expected from the collaborators and by the market that the company aims to produce their goods for.

Under this new perspective, any investors, new partner or professional who intends to work on the company's ranks must necessarily raise fundamental questions about this company, intending to determine its conditions of long-term survival, just like the level of trust and effort each collaborator must put in it. This questions will aid to understand the *corporate me* this company shares, fundamental to provide security and raise awareness to both collaborators and investors as to why is necessary to sweat the shirt, work, invest time and energy in this company, instead of other.

Among the main questions, I bring attention to the following, which can be made in sequence or randomly:

- Why this company exists?
- What are this organization's values?
- What is their business differential?
- Who are its competitors?
- What are the demanded functional competences?
- The company intends to be better, more efficient and more profitable?
- What this company to make the world better?

These questions are essential on the conduction of any project, in both professional and personal life, and whoever provides the best answers will certainly pass on more stability to business and careers, and they will hardly go bankrupt and ask the government's unemployment insurance benefits in a short period. Still, by knowing the shared world company's vision about their business, the professionals will feel safer by aligning their own goals to the institutional goals, producing a synergy that goes beyond the professional know-how.

Is fundamental to know why a company must exist and what its business differentials are. This question relates directly to the market this company intends to build or conquer, which is the main reason it exists at all, and should be bound to the actions that will sustain the complete organizational structure and the interaction with its clients, investors and society in general.

The modern consumer's market have become extremely demanding regarding services and products. A product is no longer expected to supplying a need, but to overcome it. At this point, the values that determine the company's operative structure become more and more relevant, as a common appeal is to demand products to be as far as possible from slavery and child labor, sustainable and without harms to the consumer's health, and that can be often remodeled in light of the consumer's will and experience, instead of the factory's operational needs.

Companies and people must have technical knowledge of the pre-operational procedures that fundament the coordinate functioning of their business, which must be on the same direction of the company's *ethos* as a productive organization who intends to be useful to society in its chain of collaboration and sustentation.

This technical knowledge links directly with the interrelated stages of the basic operational cycle, which are defining goals, planning strategy and building the necessary structure to assure its functioning. The well-defined alignment between strategy, structure and coordinated execution is what allows organizations to efficiently achieve their goals of their business plan. The organizations who could not properly define their goals, strategy nor structure easily tend to have difficulties and, after five years, will the most likely to confirm the failure statistics.

To be better, more efficient and more profitable is already a philosophical question for modern organizations, who search to offer continuously cleaner, more valuable services with better operational practices today available. Nonetheless, to be better and more productive, the more essential functional competences are changing quickly and often business fail by the lack of skill of managers who cannot align their productive structures to the required competences, the base of the realization of the organization's goals, which can be translated as efficiency in the organizational process, commercial and financial, also on the chains of interactions created.

To achieve efficiency it is necessary every process' "coordinators", who assure the organic and healthy functioning of the enterprise, to assume a highly technical posture also made structurally available daily routines and proceedings that will generate more safety, coordination, collaboration and efficiency to the management process. The simple offer of products and competitive and innovative services is no longer enough to maintain a healthy company if the organizational structure does not produce, on the same pace, financial results to circulate the invested capital. It means that to remain alive and competitive, it is not only necessary to satisfy the consumers' expectations, but to earn enough revenue to cover operational costs, to pay off the investors and collaborators, to pay the due taxes required by the State and eventually to contribute to a fair social cause.

In business world, financial health is one of the main factors to the maintenance of a company on the long term. And efficient management of the account allows it to schedule investments, acquire assets, exclude competitors via assimilation and gather the necessary resources to implement its policy of technological enhancement and innovation. The management of the financial flow is one of the main issues on any organized enterprise who asserts the practices of good administration, and directly determines the potential of the business overall. It must obey a cyclic program where the investment reverts to revenue, to be applied on new investments to obtain more revenue, and so on.

Another relevant issue to the continuous competitive safety is the policy of investment and technological innovation of the company, referring to the organic or mechanic transformations it tends to acquire over the time, in reason of the external environmental changes or internal business decisions, or the economic system as a whole.

The two main economic theories more widely accepted about the determining factors of the technical changes that propel the companies' to enhance their technological processes, products and services are known as *technology push* and *demand pull*. The latter considers it is after the demands of the consumers (market) for specific products and services that companies must improve their technological basis, adapting to the presented requests. Meanwhile, the former considers that the *technological route itself, the scientific advances and industrial R&D activities lead the technological progress.*[21]

Most theorists nowadays sustain that the technological impulses are determining to the progress of the production system, and consider undeniable that science produces new knowledges, which will be used on the technological innovations that enhance the level of production. Nonetheless, it is also undeniable that nowadays, the necessity of technological innovation imposed into products and services, or even means of production, are a result of the needs of the consumers and the trajectory its consumption presents. An example is what happened to the banking sector on pioneering the availability of remote access to services and financial transactions, influenced by external factors, mostly the difficulty of mobility on the larger cities around the world and the required safety on the process of coming and going to these institutions.

Finally, another issue that eventually can take admirable, profitable and innovative companies to the ledge of the abyss is the management of the power system, especially in companies under familiar management. Any enterprise whose management is a responsibility of more than one professional must make sure that both managers have in mind the necessity to profit and generate results, instead of the search and quarrels for power. This is a job for professional politicians, whose "annihilation" of finances and social results of the State for the sake of the insane and exaggerated attachment for power will condition the individual to act and live on an "individual life", whose main trait is the need to own.

This little previous analysis can be done by any professional who seeks to work in a safer, more organized and more coordinated manner, aiding to understand the level of organization, health and efficiency a company where this professional intends to work, what are its priorities and potentials and where both want to be on the next vacations. Others, even though disorganized or misguided, can offer excellent learning opportunities, serving as challenge and motivation to those who can offer a possibility of restructuring and reorganizing its management process, who intend to risk more in challenging ventures, and who do not care too much about their next vacations or holidays.

High Mobility on Jobs: Do They work?

On the American movie Year One[22], 1999, directed by Harold Hamis and starred by the iconic comical actor Jack Black, one of the first scenes consists in a slacker character named Zed (Black) who claims he does not intend to be a simple hunter or collect fruits and roots on that tribe, which were the only professions on the tribe.

This simple and comic scene portraits a reality that lingered for most of the human history, where there were no real options to choose a career or profession, and the highest "employment" rate were of the hunt and fruits. In that world, nobody dreamt of being a fashion designer or a professional musician. Some could even develop a fashionable piece of clothing, or sing a nice song around the bonfire, but these events were only preceded by the wish of mating with a desired female, or the simple wish to entertain other members of the bunch for fun, but never as a professional career as a singer or designer around ancient world.

The process of Sedentism and the continuous coexistence around larger amounts of people in fortified towns and villages allowed the beginning of the labor diversification and the rise of the first specific professions, like agriculture, security, herding, weapon's and jewel's manufacturing, woodworking and the commercial activities conducted by those who dedicated themselves to trading goods for a common value, like gold or money. Even in this new setup, most people still worked on agriculture, cattle raising or security of the cumulated wealth, where only a minority dedicated themselves to commercial or artisanal activities, and an even smaller minority dedicated themselves to culture, arte, religion and occasional literature.

On this long period when professions multiplied, the work relations were enforced through sheer brute force, violent pressure, punishment for crimes or even forced labors through slavery, in a system where most free men followed their parents' professions and the slaves were used to fulfill their owners' needs, including sexually. Meanwhile, women provided home support for their husbands and were directly responsible for their children's and younger family member' education and culture, given that in patriarchal societies, it was always the female role to leave their family in favor of the husband's.

For thousands of years, absolutely most people learned their work technics in the household, where, after the theoretical learning, they would conduct the family's business, provide the family's sustain and direct their successors' education.

The advance of industrialism in both capitalist and the proclaimed socialist societies changed the route of knowledge of people from a profession similar to their parent's, and created an array of specific careers totally apart from their ancestor's . Besides, the great industries created many general professions, lacking a specific learning and operating identity, aimed at feeding strong arms to the daily mechanical process of the assembly line, while the worker's brain was supposed to be left home, so he could behave according to the process and instructions the machines required.

Nowadays, there are many more professions to choose, as there are many other possibilities of professions yet to be created, especially those who meld traditional areas like computer's or informational engineering with nano and biotechnologies. However, in the current world, regular and formal jobs are becoming more and rarer, professions no longer pass down from father to son and specific careers are becoming more strict and limited to certain areas, being often discouraged. This new, careerless environment with many different professions helped to radicalize the idea of often rotating jobs, in a system where those who rest too long on the same company performing the same function are seen as lax, and end up losing the ability to compete for the best posts in other organizations or even in their faithful company.

This new environment led many people to believe firmly that to changing jobs is necessary at least in a determined period, from four to six years, for instance, or at least that they can vertically rise on their career within the same company in a similar period. However, deep down, is it really worthy to invest in the belief that those professions who remain so long in a profession are being left behind? Is this necessity of mobility in employment the same for every profession and career? Or even, is there any correlation between this necessity of changing jobs and the new robotic and technological changes that companies are implanting within their operational and management systems?

Most HR professionals will say yes, in a blink. But considering that everything in the modern world is relative, besides time and space, a few important considerations, especially because in some careers, after a few years it becomes impossible to revert, like the Academic and Military. Besides, many professionals that develop exclusive abilities allow themselves to change jobs or careers whenever they desire, despite the time they invested in a certain situation, unafraid of curricular changing or invalidations.

To enlighten this affirmation, I always refer to the soccer star Lionel Messi, who is currently on the same team for 15 years, performing the same job. In his case, he could certainly change to any other soccer team, or marketing company, anywhere in the world, and certainly, he would be well received and well paid in his new venture. He, as well as some professionals of different areas, have an overwhelmingly specific differential, almost impossible to reproduce by other people, even in similar conditions. This example could be extended to the teaching area, where many teachers expend their entire professional lives working, researching and developing the same contents, in the same areas and institutions, without caring for alternatives careers outside their developing projects. Especially because knowledge is always in expansion, granting more quality and specificity to those who dedicate themselves longer to a common area. It is equally possible to apply the same concept to professionals of the medical area and researchers who dedicate themselves into analyzing human, social, physio-chemical and religious conditions, besides many other areas-ends whose specific work subject cannot be understood without huge amounts of dedication.

In this aspect, it is possible to assert that the more specific and exclusive is the level of applied knowledge to any wealth or knowledge generation process, the harder it is to replace personnel, because knowledge is a product of the owner's direct appropriation.

Another fundamental question is the existence of countless levels of sophistication and performance criteria for companies, brands, institutions and academic/professional entitling, whose acquisition, participation and collaboration is, by itself, a symbolic qualification for the professionals who work on it, and serve as reference for the whole industry. For instance, who worked at NASA, Microsoft, Google, Honda, ITA or EMBRAER possess a symbolic "title" much more relevant than people who worked in companies that are yet to become reference on their fields. It allows such professionals to enjoy a higher level of employment than many of their competitors, even if they remain years performing the same job, in the same company.

Symbolic entitlement is extremely important for HR managers in many companies, who would rather add to their ranks candidates who display a larger curricular value, even though they cannot perform the skills as well as their resumes indicate. On the other hand, many professionals possess a high level of "know-how" and a "know-what"[23], but cannot compete for the best spots while not having a desired symbolic qualification from the high profile, most admirable companies on the area. Symbolic entitlement is, thus, one of the most important differentials when changing jobs in most areas, and it is maybe one of the HR manager's greatest mistakes.

In many conversations I had with excellent professionals who are losing space in the market, every single one complained and recognized that companies would rather hire unexperienced professionals with a more specific, high-level academic formation. Only after that, the company will try to imprint the specific "know-how" and "know-what" appropriate to these professionals' organizational process, after the values the company consider more relevant, especially when it comes to the management process, which is more peculiar in its own way.

Undeniably, there are still countless of professions and professionals whose long time in the same company will not interfere on the value the market will attribute to they, neither will diminish their ability of professional relocation, when necessary. Nevertheless, in many careers (especially in basic services, like surveillance and cleaning) which demand a lesser degree of capacitation, the remaining in the same company or job for too long can be damaging, granting a negative symbolic value to the professional's career.

In this new work environment, companies seek professionals with a good technical qualification, who can develop differential skills within the company's environment and can easily work as a team, motivated to continuously keep learning. Their main goal must be develop essential skills to manage, lead and motivate groups of people to a common goal, the institution's organizational objective. People without ambition, relaxed in their comfort zone, usually cannot deal satisfactorily with incertitude, changes and risk-taking situations, traits determining to the modern age and to the company's own competitiveness.

After a certain level of management activities, besides the said requirements, it is still fundamental that the professional is able to teach, accordingly to the organizational needs. In a sense, to remain a long time in an organization only reinforce the commitment to the process of corporative education that the company develops, highly valuing the managers who dedicate themselves to such activities, and considering that only people create and share knowledge. Many professionals who stay a long time in a company or job, and cannot value their curriculums to a higher level, sin mainly by the lack of interest in becoming leaders committed to the corporative education and who are not willing to share their "know-how" with a team, a knowledge that is only differential when shared, reinvented and expanded.

Another profoundly negative point for many professionals is their level of institutionalization, when professionals become hostage to a specific process without criticism, binding them to daily processes and routines, a limiting stress factor to the improvement of a company who could hire them. Besides, it can indicate a certain level of relaxation regarding the expansion of their own career, demonstrating to the market that those professionals can only grow up to a certain level, and when reached they become demotivated to keep learning and encouraging their colleagues.

Not to forget that high work mobility exists both for the people who are ruthlessly fired by the companies, as for the companies that a client can dismiss without a blink, because work is one of the most dynamic economic factors in the world, and nobody should be forced to keep executing a work they see no sense in doing. Regardless of the environment, the good professionals can adapt their work style to the operational routine of the company and to their own know-how, while institutionalized, demotivated professionals will take any task without questioning, only with interior complaints and without commitment into adding something useful to the organization.

Thus, professionals aimed at growing, learning, expanding and building something much more than what the company asks (and pays for) before anything, must ask themselves what can be done to improve the routine of the work process, and what can be added to grant more efficiency, dynamism and stability.

The professionals disciplined to the point they all search how to enhance the process of work and management can dismiss any company they want to, because they will always have somewhere else to work. However, those who cannot build the conditions to improve or innovate themselves will prove the company made a sore decision in hiring them, and have no reason to keep demanding their services, as the lack of response directly interferes in the company availability to keep around someone who is only doing "the best they can". To be productive, proactive and willing to take new challenges, even if facing outdated conditions and tools that most companies are trying evade as soon as possible. Outdated tools and relaxed people can be replaced anytime, anywhere.

People who work their entire lives without offering nothing new, innovative and authentic are certainly only after a reasonable salary, to live in peace, without concern for the idea that anything can be better, always. However, as stated in the beautiful lyrics in the song "I Believe", by R.E.M., only the reflexive knowledge and disciplined practice can achieve perfection; "Perfection is a fault, and fault lines change". As perfection is always changing, so must we.

High mobility employment, far from being an absolute rule, poses two very distinct edges: to those who always study and work looking for perfection – like Messi – who do not care about how many days or years they rest in the same post, in the same company, and would only change jobs for challenge and personal satisfaction; and to those who relax and take the world as it is, or "how it is supposed to be", being constantly forced to look for new jobs or careers to fit other's perspectives, with no condition of personal growth nor realization.

Work and Grow as a Team, Always

Human beings, conscious of their existence and carrying within thousands of files stored on their personal memories, connecting them to their past results, has developed a high capacity of programming its actions and trying to systematically coordinate its execution according to a plan. Following this logic, everything would be perfect, beautiful and wonderful, except for a few things, if what we intended did not collided daily with whatever the world or the "system" or the collective needs of the State want to collective produce for itself. Nonetheless, the world where we live is also a conscious living being, and as such, possesses a memory, an existential plan and a huge desire to achieve its planned or random goals, with no necessity to consult us and regardless the feeling of guilt it would cause in many people according to their ideal worlds.

In the fight between what I individually want and what collectively can be done by a group of people who need me to execute shared tasks attributed according to individual skills, the group's – or world's – goal is more relevant, taking a huge advantage over individual desires and projects who do not fit precisely within the gears of life's processes, company's processes or the processes of the community surrounding theses individuals.

Obviously, nobody is oriented or forced to abandon their sincere wishes and goals because the world does not allow a lonely, independent lifestyle. Actually, it is a necessity, or even more comfort, in the alignment between aimed dreams and possibilities offered, built or legated anywhere, anytime, by a group of people who although individually different, share the same system of truth, the same values and a sense of cooperation and discipline. In this aspect, the local social structures, companies, universities and armies better suited to collaborative work are always in advantage, especially in situations where the difficulties are intense and possibilities of thriving are low and remote.

Apart from what people of the modern genus *Homo sapiens* believe, the Nazis asserted that people where the problem, and as such, by eliminating people the problems would go always. Obviously the Nazis fell much faster than the problems they created, like this deeply damaging and erroneous statement they created to justify their heinous crimes. Actually, in the long human history, the solution to problems was always people, encouraged to collaborate with other people to search for efficient solutions to problems who transcended the normal, and that could encourage other people to collaborate with more people, aligning their same ideas instead of dividing and ruthlessly slaughtering them.

It is stated that the great roman general Julius Caesar said and practiced the *Divide et Impera* policy – divide and conquer – for he knew that people who stood together, sharing a collective ideal, could not be conquered without heavy losses by the great Roman army, and in order to weaken their enemies it was necessary to break whatever made them united and discipline with promises, threats or bribery.

As remarked along this book, knowledge can only be created by individuals decided to do it consciously and by people willing to collaborate with others to build a better world. Even in a world dominated by the high-stake corporations and computer technologies, it is worthy considering that corporative organizations cannot create knowledge on their own, without individuals[24] who empower them, and without the great ideas that ingrain these individuals' lives.

Nowadays, a significant part of the work process in any corporation can be performed anywhere outside the company's walls, through computers connected to the internet, producing a level of professional interaction between people only for changing data and information, without any physical or emotional contact between the parts involved, linked only by the specific function of said work process. This remote, fractured work environment widened the difficulties in interaction for countless professionals, who can no longer work with teams composed by diverse people, as different as chalk and cheese. Human contact became very limited thanks to the extreme utilization of communication devices that require no need to use or perceive the voice, the touch, and the improvised gestures in an interaction which brought people together in leisure moments for thousands of years.

Modern offices are full of stories, where the people who live and work in the same physical environment would much rather communicate via instant messages and "digital caricatures" instead of touch, gesture and voice. This new form of dry, silent communication with pre-made electronic texts and images goes against that expressed decades ago in the famous, beautiful song "The Sound of Silence", by Paul Simon, where he spoke about emptiness and solitude people feel living in a world where physical contact is not important anymore, and sometimes even seen as offensive, and silence is a dominant imposition.

> And in the naked light I saw
> Ten thousand people, maybe more
> People talking without speaking
> People hearing without listening
> People writing songs that voices never share
> And no one dared
> Disturb the sound of silence.[25]

Seems like this silence disturbance is a curse and absolutely unnecessary in families, offices and social remote networks. It appears that only in capitalist, highly profitable churches, the silence is broke by the mad screams of preachers and miraculous healers, who express in a coordinated, passionate unison a moving "give us more money, brothers in Jesus Christ".

Many good things born a work environment, and many friendships and sincere relationships are built after such interactions who are losing its strength in a sedentary workplace, individually paced, especially in the more modern environments where the texts are standard, pages are typed and displayed in archives public to intern sharing, without specific addressees.

Without a doubt, one of the biggest challenges to every manager nowadays is to efficiently coordinate the work of a team with diverse professionals, with diverse personalities and low levels of personal interactions who may consider that intern competitiveness is relevant and necessary somehow. This is troubling not only for the organization but also for the professionals who intend to grow in their careers, as teamwork requires much more than technical skills, cordiality and specific abilities. These factors are important and necessary, but in certain efficiency levels, people need something above knowledge, skill and proactive attitudes to guide the more relevant aspects of knowing and doing, the capacity to fearlessly share, the disposition to cooperate with close people without second thoughts and the comprehension that the ends do not justify the means.

Managers who assume the condition of leader keep reinforcing continuously to their collaborators that the workplace grows and consolidates through shared, inclusive, communicative, solidary and honest relationships between those who compose it, and it is possible to produce and work much more efficiently in teams composed by people with diverse graduations, various skills and different personalities, enabling a clearer comprehension of reality. It is essential that leaders work hard to build a healthy work environment where people respect, value and include each other as parts of the larger results the institution can achieve over time.

Many legends of the Antiquity describe the conquers and gigantic achievements of a single person in a moment of their lives, which are absolutely fake or only partially true because in human history, it is practically unheard of glorious facts resulting from the exclusive work of one single being, isolated and pompous in a world apart from the rest, waiting for an opportunity of showing value and strength to the weak and oppressed.

In the tales of Sumerian, Greek and Roman cultures, especially, most of the achievements were directly gods or demigod's work, or the result of god's help to a few chosen men, like Gilgamesh, Hercules, Perseus and Achilles. In the Middle Ages, with a pronounced reduction in the number of available gods to work for us, the most fantastic deeds were performed by kings and warriors, holy men or women possessed by the evil forces. For instance Joana d'Arc, who as a warrior woman in an area dominated by brute men, was charged, condemned and burned alive and virgin for the practice of witchcraft and only centuries later would become a hero, saint and worthy of cult and adoration for her bravery and patriotism uncommon to the ladies of her time.

The accounts of Noah building an ark to save humankind from extinction, Moses defeating the Pharaoh and freeing the Jewish slaves from the Egypt, Julius Caesar conquering Gaul, as registered in his old-best-seller *Comentarii de Bello Gallico* or Clovis I unifying the franks, St. Peter building the Catholic Church, Cabral conquering Brazil, Deodoro da Fonseca proclaiming the Republic and Ajuricaba as the great Amazon warrior who rebelled against the Portuguese, are not real. But they certainly serve a purpose, aimed at producing some reality the chroniclers and writers of the antiquity wanted to preserve. Or simply to entertain their neighbors.

It must be considered that it is extremely hard to build grand oeuvres alone by any means possible, and certainly these stories seek to simplify and mystify a much different reality. It is much more coherent to consider that none of these conquers resulted from a single person's spectacular actions, because in human history all of the major achievements came from a group of people who proposed to do things differently, from an idea or a major necessity, under specific conditions that encouraged them to make their dreams become a concrete reality. The heroes that in fact existed were admired leaders who after intense efforts managed to conquer respect for their clear proposes, coordinating numerous teams of ordinary people who believed in a common goal achievable by doing their tasks as commanded by said leaders.

Actually, in order to value the groups that made a difference these stories should be told as: Noah coordinated the team that built the Ark; Moses headed the group of slaves who brightly dealt with the Pharaoh for the freedom of the Jews; Julius Caesar was the commander of the armies who indexed Gaul into the Roman Empire and Deodoro was only the moral choice to those who saw the decay of the Brazilian monarchy as an obstacle to the progress of the country and its underdeveloped population.

These people were ahead and new how to lead in an efficient manner in order to achieve many common goals, in a process of hard execution. They cannot be disqualified as heroes in their conquests, or unbound from their deeds, in parts, though it is undeniable that their greatest achievement was not the deed itself, but the ability to convince and encourage others to follow them, value their leadership, trust their knowledges and believing that their skills would be enough to achieve a complete victory, as a group. Besides, if these events were conducted by a single individual, isolate, who took every risk and conducted alone the control of necessary actions, they would most likely never been achieved and these heroes would not even exist. Considering still that the Antiquity was a world of intense use of labor force for any project, it is even more evident that every attempt to fight against the *status quo*, the order and the power could only be managed by the structural cooperation of many disciplined people, organized around the same goal.

In conclusion and above all, the greatest success of these heroes was their capacity to lead in a steady, efficient manner, a group of people with common purposes and ideals, coordinating their actions, creating whatever needed, improving what could be improved and making the world they intended to live after tireless work.

Why Companies Need Me?

Increasingly, companies are needing fewer workers to perform many tasks and routine operational functions that can be replaced by computerized or computer systems much less problematic than normal human beings. Thus, many professionals today are competing in the labor market against themselves, against other workers and, especially, against autonomous and robotized systems and machines that can perform almost all the corporate tasks of the present time. Never before in human history, machines and systems have been programmed to perform so many tasks instead of men and women fit for work. This has become an increasingly worrying social problem, since people without jobs or work do not earn sufficient income to grant the means necessary for their existence with life and dignity, amidst an increasingly wealthy, prosperous, inhuman and unequal world

In the old times - as my grandma used to say - machinery and tools were only auxiliary means, efficient to perform countless tasks that needed more than the human intellectual skill, and essential to perform heavier, repetitive and more accurate jobs. Nowadays, machinery and tools are adapted to perform any task, non-stop, automatically, independent of flesh and bone and brain humans' intervention. Besides, there are machines who started to reproduce quite similarly the intellectual human capacities, in executing tasks that demand analysis of countless variables simultaneously, or aimed at performing complex connections between isolated conditions. As such, people who intend to maintain a high level of employability must display some essential differentials, that companies need to remain efficient and competitive over time, abilities that are not easily replaceable for logic systems or chain interactions operated by Artificial Intelligence.

Obviously, most of the important skills and knowledge level required to perform organizational work are still performed by intelligent and emotional people whose skills are designed to interact efficiently with corporate production and management systems. But the widespread belief that new logical technologies enable large scale revenue and increased productivity led companies and governments to increasingly invest in autonomous systems aimed at improving the operational capacity of organizations along the decrease in the need to hire personnel to perform the same tasks as computer systems can, in a continuous and progressive process, have led many intellectuals to assert that we are really entering the age of the end of employment, at least in the way we know about jobs and careers.

Another relevant fact that directly affects the labor market is that the human population is aging later and in many countries, healthier and more sober, enabling a stretch in many professionals' labor years. These professionals longer in a company or for display in the market, resulting in many governments' rise in the retirement age to near 70 years old, as to reduce the impact in the social security systems and prevent these benefits from being cut down. This process tends to inevitably raise the unemployment rate among the younger workers and those who are about to enter the market:

> In Brazil, for instance, the total number of years of labor is around 37.1 in 2010 according to the institution. Thus, a 15 year old in 2010 would be expected to spend 37.1 years as labor force along his life, should he not be submitted to the risk of mortality before retiring.[26]

Rise in unemployment in response to the introduction of new technologies and workplace reorganizations, aligned with the stretch in the years the average worker must remain active, will have a gigantic impact in the labor market and careers in a close future. It will be relevant to those who intend to keep their jobs answering these questions: Why companies, governments and consumers need to hire my services? What are my differential skills, desired by them when hiring?

Why society needs me?

At a given moment in human history, the answer to that question would be simply because organizations and government need people to carry out continuously the tasks in their production, distribution, management, and service processes. Alternatively, people are hired because of their knowledge and skills necessary and essential for developing whatever society needs, builds or intends to build.

Nowadays, however, these are no longer the most important or meaningful answers to these questions. The most urgent need of many companies became the acquisition of automated technology, artificial intelligence and more efficient machines that can add more value to the business and to the brand became essential for the development, organization and control of what they do or intend to do with more quality in an increasingly accelerated dynamics. The development of the technological base has always been a central issue for every corporation and government, and in addition to competition for markets and consumers, there is even greater competition for the development of productive technologies, rights and patents that enable financial returns to companies, on a global scale and without labor costs or problems.

Many people look within themselves and may not find the right answers to many personal and professional issues. Many others may be looking for some coaching service that could guide them about their career and life, or even prefer to believe in miraculous and supernatural solutions that will come through prayer and penitence. However, professionals who fail to produce a coherent and sincere answer to these questions are starting to face serious problems in their careers, which can become even more serious if they do not identify the possible solutions to circumvent this situation and how to continue to be useful to companies, governments or their own community. In this world, innumerable technologies are being created precisely to eliminate or reduce failures, mistakes, imperfections, untruths and emotional considerations that often affect humans and hamper the routine of organizations, even if this search for the reduction of errors and losses, eliminate thousands of jobs around the world.

Long ago, I made those same questions to a professional of a major company in Manaus' Industrial Park, and he answered that the corporation needed him because he was the only one in his sector who knew how to operate a control system in a certain process, and should he be fired, the company would lose large sums of resources until they managed to reestablish the process. Obviously, I disagreed with that statement, and told him sincerely that he was profoundly wrong, because process and control systems executed in any device are easily adaptable to other processes, other systems or even other people, if their capacity of acquiring new knowledges were encouraged. Still, no companies hold control over the life and routine of their employees, but over their own processes, especially the logical ones, they can achieve almost absolute control. It is impossible to believe that a single employee would be an obstacle between the level of control an enterprise exerts over an essential process and the managers who define the company's course of action.

It is difficult to speculate about the functioning and limitations of the future labor market, when an array of AI systems and countless computer software take control over the operations and management of production flow in many organizations, or the taxation, surveillance and electoral systems in the governments. It is even harder to predict what will happen to a social system where people and dreams were built upon the basis of organization for labor and jobs. The answers nowadays diverge between absolute chaos like on world's end Hollywood movies and the possibility of constructing a world where work is residual, leisure and family are the most important activities in a peaceful, global community.

Even harder still is to define safe limits to how much can technology control our lives, our work process and our own intimacy. Undeniably, even living in a world where artificial intelligence technologies and systems become important in everyday life in most advanced societies, people will remain important and valued on work and leisure activities, culture and socialization. On the other hand, in a world dependent of technological intervention in almost all aspects of life, even "emulating" human knowledge, many professionals and numerous occupations will lose value and importance, as technical and moral barriers limiting the use of artificial intelligence and robotic systems in many fields of human labor are beginning to break and be accepted as the natural and inevitable actions of the development of mankind. At this moment, where people are important, but professions and careers may no longer be more powerful, responding in a secure and expanded way: why do companies and a society need me? Where my knowledge and my work can be useful in the lives of people, governments and companies?

Another relevant factor to any professionals who intend to maintain a good employability level is to be able to perceive where careers and jobs are migrating to, what are the relevant qualifications in that field and how can they become an excellent professional choice to society, seeking knowledge, skills, attitudes, values and intelligence essential to performing any role, in any company.

As stated before, it is hard to assert accurately what will happen to the labor market. By analyzing the results of a quick research I made into national and multinational companies' websites for trainee or internship programs[27] it is possible to figure out some of the main professional traits these enterprises require.

To every job vacancy the mains prerequisites were superior education, complete or about to complete, possibility of working outside the city, fluency in the English language (about 90% of the vacancies required advanced level). Courses like Business Administration (90%), Economy, Engineering (80%) and Accounting (75%) offered most of the vacancies, followed by Marketing (51%) and IT (43%). Some of the companies offered specific posts in finances, distributed between Economy and Accounting areas.

An important requirement in the recruitment of these recent graduates was at the initial level of technical qualifications, especially in relation to English language fluency, requiring a high level because most of these companies compete in worldwide markets and employ workers from multiple nationalities. Nowadays companies operate through a global production plant, aligning supply of raw materials, input processing and labor through globally integrated logistics systems, to be produced wherever the companies possess greater comparative and competitive advantage. And this global plan, operated by a multitude of professionals of multiple nationalities, requires efficient fluid communication, with English as a common language in any part of the world. Still, in order to work in a global company, the professional must be able to live and to think in an environment composed of heterogeneous teams, where the contracting company demands from the professional a sense of mutual cooperation and the unquestioned confidence that the enterprise is the worker's true world, in terms of vision, and the worker's only home, in terms of physical presence, since wherever the company intends to be present and necessary, they must be able to go as well, integrating themselves to the organizational processes in a shared and unique form, as sung in the song "Wherever I May Roam", in the Black Album of the group Metallica: "Where I lay my head is home"[28]. In addition to all the technical qualities, practical skills and proactive attitudes that companies want to find in the applicants, they also require a higher level of dedication and the professional must learn to be multilingual, multicultural, multiracial, multifunctional, multi-procedural, multi-structural and multi-spatial, in a multidimensional, volatile, uncertain and extremely complex work environment.

The careers and the labor market are heading towards a global environment, and it is necessary for those who wish to keep their jobs to realize how to fit in quickly in this new world dynamics, shared in international networks of interaction and cooperation. Those who cannot must look for coaching services urgently, before it is even harder to compete in a high level and before the only plausible course of action is recycling, a moment when the worker try to catch up to countless new devices that went by, with the hope to turn them into something new, ready to be reused.

Working in the Age of Knowledge

To live and to work in the modern age, above all, requires professionals who can perceive that changes in life are continuous, and that is why it is necessary to develop the ability to keep always learning. Besides, the knowledge era needs people who can be creative and innovative, who can think differently and build after their differences something new and necessary to a group, with or without financial feedback. Another relevant factor is that the mental capacity to connect to various simultaneous process, linking the essence of the available knowledge and the use of organizational technologies and computational interactivity, in environments where the preponderant factors will be mutual cooperation an professional sharing of whatever can be useful to strengthen the links between a group or idea. Certainly, those who achieved these abilities, in lifestyle and work, and who know how to share what enrich them, are much fitter to trail the best paths in promising careers, and to fight for the best spots in global companies.

Stephen Covey wrote extensively in his oeuvres about the habits that typify the modern workers and allow them to become more efficient, proactive and creative. He believes that the relation between knowledge and continuous learning is one of the central issues for modern professionals and to understand it correctly allows them to acquire the ability to work, act and compete for the best jobs, as:

> This Information Age is transforming so rapidly into the Knowledge Worker Age that it is going to take continual investment in our own education and training to stay abreast. Much of this will be done by the school of hard knocks, but people who see what is happening and who are disciplined will systematically continue their education until they acquire the new mind-set and the new skill-set required to anticipate and accommodate the realities of the new age.[29]

The ability to acquire new knowledge became the core of the professionals who maintained a high degree of employability and are nowadays, in a large scale, the most useful ones to companies and governments alike. In this new liquid modernity[29], one of the main issues is the high level and speed of technical updates and innovations on products, daily reinvented in what modern sociology calls reflexive modernization.

In the past, management, procedures, tools and intern processes of the companies kept a reasonably long balance, without constant technological changes and adaptations over time that would require the worker to continuously keep learning in a fast pace within shorter short periods, and neither the tools and methodologies. Ever since the moment there was a progressive transformation on global productions, associated to the process of technological enhancement and the introduction of computer technologies, the need for "technical updates" became essential and justifiable as the core of the work process. The innovations and continuous changes became paradoxes to everyone at such a fast pace of updates, and people are obliged to acquire minimum conditions to a permanent professional development, as a mean to be always "updated" with the required demands of their new work process and new ways of thinking and organizing it. Nowadays, the human necessity of "routinely 'keep in touch' with the grounds of what they do as an integral element of doing it"[31] became much more intense, and the main basis of getting things done in modernity are heavily integrated to the logical, computational systems of high operational capacity, which are continuously updated and remodeled.

As already argued, traditional assembly lines required more physical strength than creative ideas from the hundreds of workers who manipulated it, besides organizational discipline, absolute obedience and unconditional acceptance of the imposed orders. Whistles dictated the pace of work, exclusively in function of time, which was the main motivation for the existence of the factories, instead of productivity, creativeness or innovative capacity. Managers measured and were evaluated purely in numerical terms: number of hours, amount of production, quantity of losses, quantity of workers, quantity of sales and amount of revenue, only in rare cases that quality factor became relevant or was considered important. In that scenario, people worked in just one process, divided over the vast assembly lines, or in the offices and administration rooms, crammed with professionals performing a single activity: counting, typing, reviewing, signing, screwing, welding, painting, tightening and filing. According to the Fordism occupational orientation, the worker was fundamental only to be inserted conditionally into a mechanized production process, through its spatial distribution in a process developed for the execution of some alienating human tasks that the machine required. People were only living parts interacting with inanimate mass-production systems. In this scenario, the conceptions of the world followed the organization of the factory, as a great mechanical gear, where humankind processed the material means essential for its own maintenance.

Nowadays, considering that life develops after intertwined and mutually shared relations of countless physical, chemical, biological and social process, this idea of "machine world" or "factory world" is completely outdated. It is hugely necessary for both professionals and companies to be able to know the very least about their various processes integrated to its production and how they are relevant in relation to other processes. It should be considered that work in a network, place or through any integrated system of computers, that can be performed by any professional who works in the larger process work, still needs people capable of connecting to other processes and work with professionals from diverse fields in order to maximize the group's results.

Modern computational systems quickly became tools to make shared work more efficient, productive and dynamic. On the other hand, those who cannot properly interact with these systems tend be on the margin of the more rewarding possibilities, in both income and comfort. In this sense, one of the workers' main traits in the modern era is their familiarity with computational devices, essential tools in every field of human activity, which allow progressively to reduce time and distance, connect ideals, enhance researches, "mix" nationalities and more important of it all, reduce costs in daily routines. As the world's resources become scarcer, avoiding waste means saving natural resources that will sustain the next generations.

Another important condition, essential for every talented professionals of the modern world, is the ability to share ideas, work and sincere relationships, in heterogeneous teams, where the openly assumed and encouraged focus is always the result of the team, and where the need for prestige, power or control over the group is strongly discouraged or becomes derogatory. The modern world is a world where everything can be shared, especially knowledge and the procedures that determine the results in a same chain of interests.

The modern world is where everything that can be shared will be, especially the proceedings that will display results in the same chain of interest. The notion that the life is an endless, high-speed wacky race, with all of its racers aware that there is only one place in the imaginary podium, where the losers will be merciless discarded, does not deserve credit when it comes to the collective work. In this aspect, there is not just one winner. Many may want to be it, but even they eventually must admit that the result of all the work is a team effort, as Isaac Newton himself remarked: If I have seen further it is by standing on the shoulders of Giants. In the best teams and companies, the most encouraged value is the collective performance, understood as the organization's *raison d'être,* and must be conducted by those who cumulate a high level of technical knowledge, creativity, sympathy and balance between personal performance and collective needs to achieve the expected results in a constantly collaborative environment, without room for competitiveness.

Finally, another important aspect is the concept of leadership, since the leaders of this new, shared work order must be over detached from the necessity to "worship" their selfish ego, isolated and isolated from others. They interact in a collaborative, not intimidating way with all of the staff, they seek to be creative, constructive and liberal always, accepting ideas and suggestions that can be added to those shared by the team and they see their team as people, as constant and potential solutions, they are someone *who encourage the others to follow their passions, and not boss them around*[32]. They have an exact notion of their role as the main facilitator to achieve the proposed institutional goals, and the ability to instill a non-hierarchical *sprit de corps*[33], making the workplace an appropriate place for the development of new ideas and complementary attitudes that create the necessary motivation and the necessary synergy to turn people into talents, and talents into result. I also believe that one of the greatest qualities of the modern leader is the ability to form other leaders, because leadership is not a natural predisposition of a few chosen by God and destined to rule the rest of the world. Leadership is a condition available and achievable to all who work, study and strive continually to deserve it, as a result of their choices and conduct, and never as a blessing received by some as a divine response or as a prophetic promise, for accumulation of prayers.

Like power systems, leadership is also exerted, and is certainly exerted more effectively by those with a higher level of knowledge, who have a high capacity for sharing ideas, and who are willing to collaborate constantly with the whole network of work, contact and support, remembering that we are only human, and nothing more. In the end, people who give their support and trust deserve to be remembered, valued and recognized. The exercise of leadership is much more than managing people; is to manage for people and with their voluntary support.

We are expanding a gigantic world, where the use of advanced technologies reached a high level that has profoundly modified patterns and methods of production, development and, above all, working. Creative and innovative people manage to reach a much more comfortable position in terms of employment and salary, and in contrast, it is required a greater capacity for learning and a reasonable level of knowledge in the main form of interaction and communication of the modern world: the computational language.

Connecting Much More Than People

The title of this chapter may sound like a corporative slogan, and it tries to express one of the main traits of human relations in modernity: the professional network workers manage to build along their career, instead of the blood and affective ties, inherited from our parents and grandparents.

The rising insertion of automatized technologies causes diminishing of the necessity of hiring people for multiple tasks, aligned with the expressive drop in the number of posts for less qualified workers, and it is making many people to give up on looking for a formal job and start working on their own. Others, however, are amplifying their networks to assure the maintenance of a safe level of employability, trusting that their organizational family, their networking, will be a major tool to keep working in a formal, highly mutating and uncertain environment.

Nowadays, intellectual capital is one of the more valued factors in the labor market, the main condition for generating knowledge, which became immensely relevant to the financial return of the corporate and governmental investments. Alongside, "human intellectual capital" is suffering increasing pressure by the introduction of logical systems, which attempt to reproduce systematically people's mental capacities, leading to the construction of a highly technical society where the introduction of technological tools, able of human reasoning, became fundamental for economic, political and social growth.

As stated before, companies build as processing units, after the development of mass-production industrial system own a privileged seat in the cities, for making possible the gathering of a large number of people in its surroundings. These people started to cultivate new interpersonal relationships outside the hearth of family, different from the families whose main occupation was livestock or farming, more dynamic in nature, sometimes even mimicking the logics of the relationships inside the factory's facilities.

As Toffler said, the "extended family" was a major trait of societies where people's life focused on farming fields, when people with distant relatives shared lands, traditions, creeds and life for generations. After the introduction of the industrial scale production, this family started to mingle, evading the glue that held it together and gradually becoming a smaller family, amplified only by connecting and relating to other smaller families, whose potential contact began initially inside the factories and offices growing around the major cities.

Progressively, families became smaller, until essentially built by father, mother and few children, and alongside the growth of an exacerbated individualism and atrophy of social relations enabled a radical change in interpersonal relations, now limited to the nuclear family and a few behavioral, political, religious or economic affinities, or tied by the prolonged coexistence in an office or factory in the industrial era. The construction of relationships based on professional affinity, named networking, enhanced work's mobility, after the managers' needs and practicality when building up teams, valuing their experiences and relations built on prior companies. It is undeniable that whenever management changes, their professional "family" comes along, hired in the new company to serve as in its operational structure.

Good or bad, building personal relationships that bring people closer to work, careers, and success in the modern world is essentially driven by the experience and professional commitment preserved throughout life, according to the affinities and values that each professional "family", or networking, develops and believes to be true and sufficient for efficient, honest and productive work. This can still be defined in what Pierre Bourdieu coined as "social capital", which is part of his theoretical schematization of symbolic power and the conditions that lead people and position themselves more fully in relation to the more disputed or restricted social functions. The larger the network of positive contacts we establish throughout our professional career, our social capital, the greater the chances of securing or improving employment and work possibilities. However, it has nothing to do with "bootlicking", where professional relations are not based on mutual respect and trust, but are reflected only in distorted and dishonest relations of power and perverse dependence on those who

Networking is a structure of essentially professional relationships, whose affinity is to ensure a better organizational efficiency through a group of people who share values, knowledge, friendship and common goals inside their new productive structures, besides mutual trust between each member of the group. This sense of trust is fundamental to keep the maintenance of this system's network, build after the professional "family" workers constructs along their lives, and those who trust must believe that their responsibilities will be executed in the expected manner, in the planned time with the available resources, as hardly someone would sincerely delegate a task to someone untrustworthy. In the same line of thought, it is possible to assert that both the affinities build by remote relationships and build after personal, friendship relations have a similar trait: the system of mutual trust, where both parts acknowledge each other and see the other as capable and deserving of trust they share among themselves, and with the other members of the group. Constructing a network of relationships and sharing intimacy takes time and requires effort, especially in acknowledging others, qualities important in determining the type and intensity of the relation intended to build.

Another issue fundamental to the functioning of nowadays' institutions, based upon trust and intimacy, is precisely the urgent need to adapt operations in remote networks of relationships and work, connected to people, companies, products and brands via the internet. The possibility of building networks has expanded enormously from the development of remote communication and connection, leaving people superficially close, even thousands of miles away, or making them approach again after dozens of years without any kind of contact.

Building friendships and solid relationships through remote interaction networks, just like maintaining personal relationships outside the companies' facilities, become more relevant the more we believe that *no matter where we were born and whatever our culture, we share a common story – the story of human origins within the more complex story of the evolution of life on the planet*[34]. Nowadays, we believe that we can effectively become a coherent global, multiracial and multicultural society, where the goals to the planet's future is commonly relevant to every group that shares this vision.

Another relevant point is that automated production systems eliminated the need for jobs in a large scale in many areas, and in a context where cultures are deeply influenced and modeled by a common value system, relationships built around work play a larger role, and tend to ensure a certain stability and a more equitable employment for people in the same networking, as they can keep producing the expected results and remain trustworthy. Also, as employment is declining even more, this professional family can slowly transform itself into a defined unit of processing, through the constitution of companies or cooperatives of production or services, whose members possess, in addition to mutual trust, a shared prior experience dissociated from a company's ranks to provide services to those who wish to hire them independently.

As labor market is redefining, that can be the best option to many professionals around the world who display a good technical level, who can work in flexible work scales and who are members of a professional "family" who develops creative solutions for people and organizations. In other works, networking will determine the construction of business and careers outside company's ranks, but keeping the same functional logic of their "relatives", as a group of people who share goals, friendship, values and knowledge assuring better organizational efficiency.

Considering that in modern societies, interaction networks are preponderant to build relationships and brotherly ties, the social networks build from work relationships will be more and more essential to assure employment and professional growth, in closed "communities" working for the same goal, assuring employment and teamwork.

P.S.

The absurd growth of relationship networks in any situation created highly profitable enterprises, granting god-like status to the company's creator. It made society desire to come close to this status certain people achieved.

From this idea, many other possibilities of sharing relationships in remote networks are trying to be created and commercialized, which may enable that the next big step for the companies who develop software for sharing data, information, friendships and relationships is offering a services that allows to share relationships with the deceased, produced from AI to emulate their behaviors and personality in order to help people to cope with the pain of those who left unexpectedly...

It would be a high-tech solution for shamanistic services practiced only in fantasy and mental terms.

To Work Well, to Live Even Better

I strongly believe is that music, as other cultural manifestations, transcend existence. I wonder quite often how the world would be like without music, theater, poetry and the ability to express feelings that cannot be quite explained by modern scientific truths. Human beings are animals that need to find a meaning for everything, from life to death. They have an even greater need to explain their own existence, in a world so complicated that, in the absence of answers, they see in the search for pleasure and happiness one of the main reasons for existence, conscious that pleasure and happiness are purely personal concepts, which only at some point or another can be collective and definitive.

There are many reasons for the continuous search for pleasure, happiness and material satisfaction that can appease an individual at a certain level. Even though many philosophical and religious systems consider the search for pleasure and happiness as "inferior" and meaningless, undoubtedly most human beings strongly believe that it is the two maximum conditions for existence.

As far as we know, most animals find happiness – or better, satisfaction – in assuring food, shelter and a mating partner, mostly. However, for most men and women, the satisfaction of essential needs, which allows their plain realization, goes far beyond eating, sleeping and mating. Biological satisfaction is only one of many variables in the equation of how each person sees happiness. To assure it, human beings created an infinity of ideas, senses, products, services, machines and tools that increases the possibilities of having joy; from eating and dressing to transportation for showing off, leisure and work.

As such, a fundamental point to men and women, one of the most important variables to assure what we know as pleasure, comfort and personal satisfaction is the capacity to work, even more important due to its increasing scarceness, limitations and instability in societies historically organized around work and production of knowledge to apply in work's process. However, the simple capacity to work does not make people happier, especially in low-qualification activities in derogatory, low-paying and degrading situations. It is hard to assume someday someone as child ever dreamt of becoming a trash collector, cleaning industrial facilities or carrying around merchandises or suitcases in airports and harbors around the world.

Although it seems exclusive to undervalued jobs, it also exists, even in a stressed manner, among professionals of more socially wanted positions, as the number of people who claims to be unhappy with their careers grew exponentially, for worrying reasons yet to be explained.

In the long humankind history, men progressively believed that the search for happiness related directly to the type of work each one performed in society and how much power one could achieve with it, granting the political jobs the status of most wanted posts. A point of view consolidate in Ancient Greece assumed that the greatest virtue was not to have to work on daily, manual activities, and the finest minds and souls should only dedicate themselves to intellectual activities, especially when it comes to learning and constructing systems that could improve the quality of life and work for the cities' free citizens. Nonetheless, for heavier jobs like farming or construction of gigantic monuments and temples to appease the ego of rulers, the work sought after was mainly slave, constituting as the primary labor force for turning the cogs of that ancient societies.

According to some, hard work began as a reality to humankind ever since God expelled us from Eden. However, this ruthless "firing" from heaven department did not cause a huge level of hard work they had to perform, for Adam only had Eve to feed, and I'm guessing they didn't need much to be happy. According to others, however, it began when the first humans started to settle down in farms and primitive villages, where the main activity was farming and tending livestock. Besides the military duty, these two occupations were the backbone of job opportunities for most people, free or slave, during most of our history. There were still a minority dedicated to commerce, and another minority who did not work, instead dedicating themselves to offering religious services in public temples around cities crowded with sinners.

Some wealthy enough people, who did not need to earn their bread and butter by shedding sweat of their faces through intense manual labor, started to dedicate themselves to the researches and studies in order to develop technical and intellectual improvements that could construct new ways of thinking, doing and organizing the world, besides understanding the phenomena that conditions life. These people did not work on the intense labor force, and instead dedicated themselves to the production of written materials and logical systems, seeking to analyze the conditions of life in society. They were philosophers, thinkers, merchants, lawmakers, poets, sorcerers and conquerors. And precisely these lazy, idle citizens who enabled the construction of modern sciences.

Life seemed perfect for societies where the slaves and their descendants provided all labor for the heaviest daily tasks until the system of exploitation of the work force based on human slavery collapsed, giving rise to the well-known feudal system. However, it retained essentially the same power relations and class characteristics of ancient societies - nobility, clergy, military and peasantry - replacing human exploitation via slavery with a more subtle type of exploitation based on honorable serfdom and, especially in Western Europe, this new system of social organization eventually reduced the immense number of ancient gods to only one, the God of the Jews.

When the model of feudal organization fell, the rising society with the intellectual availability of those who dedicated themselves to studies instead of work started to structure ideas, process, machinery and tools that could mitigate the hardships of people's work, allowing them to perform tasks in a smaller timespan and through a milder effort. Consequently, they could enable the freedom of workers gifted with the new inventions, to use their newly free time in a more constructive and pleasant way.

The unstoppable search for new technologies partially seeks to grant the building of tools, productive process, mechanisms and models more efficiently, easier and less overwhelming for the practice of labor, which is the exact opposite of leisure for many people. Instead, in many senses, it did not happened entirely. In many professional areas, the introduction of new tools and modern, efficient systems caused a growth in the volume of work, and stretched the time necessary to perform it correctly, like in law and consultant offices aimed at remote consultations. Nowadays, just like in the ancient Egypt, there are people who, after a stressful workday, come back home only to eat and faint due to exhaustion, to wake up again to another tiring workday with little to no time to spare for leisure with family.

Nonetheless, in some areas work really became milder, cleaner and more intellectual, allowing its fast execution in a more definitive way than possible decades ago. For instance, in management activities, due to a great number of workers dedicated to deal only with data and instead of moving workers to where the information is, its preferable to move the information to where the workers are[35], leaving a larger amount of time for people to dedicate themselves to leisure and to use some of their idle time to develop intellectual and learning activities, in order to improve their work performance.

In his classic book "Creative Idleness" (l'ozio creativo), Domenico de Masi stands for the idea that every time not dedicate to work, like studying, traveling and leisure contributes much more to people's performance in work than the time spent in work itself. Mainly, because in the modern world, work is essentially intellectual or robotic, and can be execute in a shorter timespan in reduced or variable conditions. It enables people to become more and more sedentary regarding work.[36]

Those professionals who can perform their works in a modern, technological environment, surrounded by efficient network-based computer systems, usually tend to enjoy a larger amount of time to develop leisure and culture activities, besides the additional time reserved to their continuous and essential process of learning.

If well enjoyed, idle time can be a powerful ally to learning and to correcting necessary to the highly intellectual work process of the modern times. It is necessary to be careful, though, as many people waste their idle time with empty activities, striped from any meaning or quality. Besides, we are every day less prone to attribute to others qualities we believe to see in ourselves, which can turn to valuable sources of learning, pleasure and love.

Referências Capítulo IV

1. **IBGE - Anuário Estatístico Brasileiro 1980**
2. Ibidem
3. Mary del Priore, **Uma breve história do Brasil**.
4. Argemiro j. Brum, **Desenvolvimento econômico brasileiro**, 16 ed. P.85.
5. ibidem p .89.
6. IBGE
7. Walter Isaacsson, **The Inovators: How a Group of Hackers, Genius and Geeks created The Digital Revolution**, 2014, p. 189
8. Zygmut Baumam, **On Education: Conversations with Ricardo Mazzeo**, p. 36.
9. IBGE, 2014
10. Ikujiro Nonaka e Hirotaka Takeuchi, **On Management Knowledge**, 2008.
11. SEBRAE 2013
12. Ibidem
13. **Pesquisa Anual de Serviços – PAS** – IBGE. 2014
14. James Collins, Jerry Porras, **Built to Last: Successful Habits of Visionary Companies**, 1994, p. 51
15. Ver Geofey Blaney , As 50 maiores batalhas
16. Fritjof Capra, **The Turning Point**, 2006, p. 260.
17. Ibidem, p. 260.
18. Ibidem, p. 260.
19. Lloyd Geering, **The World to Come: from Christian Past to Global Future,** 2011, p. 111.
20. Ikujiro Nonaka e Hirotaka Takeuchi, **On Management Knowledge**,
21. Carolina Marchiori Bezerra, **inovações tecnológicas e a complexidade do sistema econômico.**
22. **Year One**, 2009, directionHarold Ramis, Columbia Pictures
23. Ikujiro Nonaka e Hirotaka Takeuchi, **On Knowledge Management**, 2008.
24. Ibidem
25. Paul Simon, 1964, Columbia Records
26. **Life Expectancy in Brazilian Labor Market**, Charles Henrique Correa Junho, 2015, Banco Central do Brasil.
27. http://exame.abril.com.br/carreira/ em 25-10-16
28. Metallica, **Black Album**, 1991, Elektra Records
29. Stephen Covey, **the 8th hab**it, 1989.
30. Zygmunt Baumman's Concept
31. Anthony Giddens, **The Consequences of Modernity**, 1990.
32. Walter Isaacson, **The Innovators: How a Group of Hackers, Geniuses and Geeks Created the Digital Revolution**, 2014, p. 379
33. Ibidem, p. 152

34. Lloyd Geering, **The World to Come: from Christian Past to Global Future**
35. Domenico De Masi, **Creative Idleness,** p. 189.
36. Ibidem

> Certainly all historical experience confirms the truth - that man would not have attained the possible unless time and again he had reached out for the impossible.
> Max Weber

V – The Being, The World and the Nothingness

The being and the nothingness sounds close to the title of the magnum opus of the great French philosopher Jean-Paul Sartre[1] who believe that human existence's main goal – in his conceptions of existence – constituted in trying to be free to live and choose without any moral, godly, ideological or cultural barrier. As himself pointed out, though, freedom bears an overwhelming weight whose bearers are the only ones responsible for their lives' results and choices, and it bothers much more than then a life without freedom because responsibility is a much heavier condition than living in a cage.

Considering that men and women are the only responsible ones for their choices and that life is not predetermined by an order from beyond this world, then each one may have conditions to create the world they desire according to their daily choices, at their best conveniences. In this aspect, despite the power systems and structures that condition life in society, we are the result of what we want to be, of what we chose to be and of what we limited ourselves to be with our daily actions and nothing else. The major result of choices synthetizes what we are today and, if we are not what we once desired it is because our choices were not adequate to achieve our goals

Faith Alone Does not Move Mountains

During almost all my life I believed in this old saying, but nowadays it seems widely distorted from the one that was a common part of the values system of countless religious cultures, , which sought in unshaken faith the certainty that miracles continuously happen, a solid foundation to sustain the necessary motivation to remain alive, trusting and safe. Nowadays, it is clearer that to operate miracles and move mountains we need not only faith but also knowledge, endurance and lots of hard work, even if in a purely intellectual level.

Along history, the belief that faith is more than anything else became a trait and a fundamentally religious condition, especially when Christianism took over the place of pagan beliefs after the assumption that Jesus said those words himself. This assertion lost its power as scientific advances started to dissect natural phenomena in simple, understandable facts and enable a more rational belief in life and in the universe, with the dominance of the scientific creed leaving little space to spiritual considerations.

Men and women, individually or organized in collectives, always tented to link themselves to some sort of cult, which at some point was appropriated by dogma and religious orders stablished as official as the only valid form of faith, imposed, practiced and displayed as real by religious corporations. By imposing to societies a common ritualistic practice, it sought to grant that everything would be attainable in this life or the next, after moral acceptance, spiritual submission and unconditional adoration of the god said religion determined as the only true one.

According to Max, the belief in God as an abstract product of human consciousness is the last breath of the oppressed, while institutional religion is the addicting oxygen through which the oppressed can breathe. To them, religious system oppressed even more those who were already beneath society who, desperate and unconsciously, accepted the creed system imposed by the theocratic state and in the process losing for a long time the understanding that the human mind is a powerful tool, as themselves for carrying this conscious mind.

We all have, from an early age, some belief system that sustains our lives and actions, making us believe that the results of our thoughts, our actions, are our bidding in our behalf, adding to us what we believe, that we seek or merely think it is possible to obtain, as health, wealth, women, wisdom, careers, or all that. According to my wise brother, to have faith is to believe in the invisible and in the impossible, and no matter what, people somehow and for some reason believe that something invisible surrounds us and connects us to our seemingly impossible goals. However, faith is much more than mere religious speculation that there is a God to every human cause, problem or solution. Faith is a condition of someone's very existence, and it has nothing to do with religious abstractions that attempt to attribute one single specific meaning, support or fundament. Faith is a human condition with ourselves, build after experiences, material and existential needs.

Ever since humankind instituted slavery as a form of violent appropriation of the other's work, official religious sought to stablish the monopoly of this system, seeking to assure that the people submitted to the forced labor system felt relieved of this burden by the expectancy of another's life enjoyment, free of the hardships of slavery and any physical or psychological suffering.

In this long process, the religious system enlarged itself and started to control almost all of the citizens' lives, surpassing the simple system of creed it initially proposed to "coordinate" until merging with peoples' existence. It became so staunchly unfair that people drift away from their individual or familiar belief and started to adopt this imposed belief, which promised to free the soul without imprisoning the body in an outdated system of material restrictions and allegedly unacceptable behaviors.

Despite the cultural and theological level each bears, three fundamental structures sustained the faith system each group preserved and developed. In this aspect, the faith in a divine God remained the biggest, and the self and consciousness, in a lesser degree, remain deeply relevant. To some, the Church (or faith collective) and its rites displayed something "real" to believe in, in the individual search for answers and solutions to daily problems, until the advance of the Age of Reason and the scientific religion.

Traditional belief claims there is a God, or gods, that can control and condition our existence, among other things, after His intentions with each one. He delivers us from occasional difficulties and helps us conduct our existence so we can enjoy a full life, rich in blessing and depending on the vision each one constructs, it can be both rich in materials as in spiritual truths. To achieve said blessings, though, there is the downside of accepting total and honestly that this God is the one and only try father of humankind, without which humans would starve in serfdom and misery in this life or the next, considering there is an afterlife.

The mechanisms that sustain human faith in an omniscient God suffered countless transformations along history, and the belief in a God that aids men and women to conquer their goals in a more and more technical, individualistic, materialistic society, helped to create the so-called retribution theology. In this system, God is essentially a guarantor for gold international credit card to those who in He believe, so they can achieve their huge and unlimited material needs, beyond their standards. And, as these material wishes are unlimited, it is asked to this God's wallet the most insane requests, from expensive luxury cars to congress' posts, always following the advertisement of being a "gift from God".

Faith in God or in a superior energy is almost fundamental to, at least, dreaming with a better, happier existence. The way faith practice turned, though, usually directed at meeting a specific material need, distorted the relationship between the humans and their creator, leaving many people miserably imprisoned to the fake promises promoted by alleged interpreters of God's will, when He would most likely be more relieved if these people started to have more faith in themselves, accepting that themselves and their minds are immensely powerful and can be the more efficient way to become who they want to be. The mind can, yet, solve many questions whose answers were sought in others, finding solutions to experiences not lived, knowledge without purpose and relationships not shared.

Every individual essentially seeks a personal, spiritual or professional, or even existential goal. However, quite often this search for meaning is external to the being, without developing and practicing a tool of interaction between the true self and the mind who controls it, through the practice of meditation, continuous reading, listening to songs or simply to the silence, turning off the world to enable a connection between oneself and what one believes to be his self.

The practice for the search of interior knowledge is healthy and fundamental to every human who has a clear purpose in life, or even to those who seek one after the discoveries produced about themselves. When Socrates said to know thyself, he certainly achieved this conclusion through the wise experience of searching inside his own interior mental universe, to find the answers (or questions) that often are not found written openly in the lines of life, nor in the Bible in a purely conventional manner. We must use our own mental dialectics to grown in peace and wisdom, and to learn continuously with ourselves, as he asserted.

Socrates was not the first nor the only to trust this much in his own mind as in an alleged collective mind one could understand as God. But, he was certainly one of the first humans to develop a method of investigation based in a repetitive model of an internal and external dialogue, known as Dialectics, from the assumption of an idea confronted with its negations until having an understanding of the truths the original ideal upheld. It changed investigation and knowledge searching forever, allowing that nowadays we have a more accurate notion that human's brain and mind are structures beyond our conscience, as many cerebral process are unconscious and happen even if unavailable in our memory.

Recent researches pointed out that our brain is a functional structure with its own life and ideas. It inhabits us, but functions specifically to some roles and intentions, independent of our desires, goals or needs. When we can connect in the same plan our minds with ourselves, often we perceive an absolute clash between what we believe to be real and what the mind perceives as true and important. This discovery of the true self produces a great disturbance in the conscious mind, who tend to develop two extreme situations and incomprehensible to most mortals: One is madness, and the other is sanctity and wisdom.

It would explain why Buddha, St. Francis of Assisi, St. Augustine, Diogenes, Socrates, St. Paul and many others who managed to connect in a more intimate level with their unconscious minds changed so abruptly their thoughts and purposes, starting to live in a world apart. They even managed to build an interior world completely different from any model of known world lived by their contemporary.

The positivist belief in human mental capacities, besides not including God in its assumptions, strongly believed in the objective rationality as the propelling force to developing human progress, and overcoming daily needs. Still, people skeptical of God's existence became more and more focused in valuing reason as a valuable asset and essential ally to building a modern world, through the production of scientific and intellectual modern materials.

The advance of the Positivist, rational, mechanic thought helped to shake the belief in the Church as a structure able to develop individual faith, and sought to dismiss the belief in an almighty God – or in any other superior force – that could relate to our existence beyond the physical, visible world. It allows the construction of a thought system strongly focused on rational and methodical understanding of human rationality's potential, and how it condition life and its purposes in a gigantic universe. This vision, aligned with countless discoveries, enabled the construction of a highly technological world, contribute with the decline in the Church's structuring force and the development of a faith based upon the individual itself, working as a valuable motivation to hard work in the search for answers and goals, planned or seen as true, for those who seek them,

Faith in oneself, or self-confidence was always a differential asset for people focused in results, more remarkable as individualism became the irreproachable religion of the modern world and people strayed from the necessity of God as the main source of faith and motivation. Besides, the social institution known as community became more of an empty environment for most people, who started do construct and cult relationships in the cold space of their own rooms through the internet.

Nevertheless, motivated, efficient and happier people develop many mechanisms of faith and personal motivation, where they believe and share their most important goals as they one day will achieve, through conciliation of skills and knowledge applied to their process of acting and working. Between these main motivations, certainly God, the human mind and self-confidence are among the most important, operated daily in actions ranging from sincere prayer to constructing a huge base of systematic and theoretical knowledge, having in mind the main condition to their faith, besides inner conversation and reflection.

Despite individual values each one may bear, or the belief each one shares, faith is fundamental to achieve our goals when well based, in a conscious and realistic manner, enabling an additional propulsion to the individual to improve his or hers confidence, self-esteem, and encourage the pursuit of whatever deemed as real and possible. However, faith and self-confidence are only positive factor who can indeed move mountains when fed by tireless disposition for working hard, objectively and efficiently. Never alone, as in the tale of the person who drowned because waited for God in person to save him after a shipwrecking, refusing the help of many boats who passed by, believing faith alone would save his life.

Failing is Easier Than Trying to Succeed

Even though this assertion is deeply true, I am sure success is the result of work and errors, and they can overcome the delusion and melancholy during the search of our dreamt goals. On the other hand, considering the large array of products and services announced on a daily basis as fascinating magical elixirs to achieve or perform almost everything, in an easier, quicker way. Many books who follow this same "philosophy" have been dedicated to teach the secrets of professional success, improvement in management techniques, the paths for personal growth and the fundamental habits for achieving goals everyone seeks, fast and easily. However, there are no magic, immediate and easy solutions to success, just as the necessary conditions and important qualities to professional or corporative success are not absolute, as nothing in this life. The construction of a good career or a happy life can be edified through many different means, even seemingly conflicting methods. The sole convergence point, common to every successful situation, is called "work".

Both Bill Gates an Steve Jobs, along their less famous partners, built companies and brands immensely admired and valued but based in opposite methods and different work and management styles, legating two powerful enterprises who compete in the same market. One of the fundamental points for both, though, besides the certainty they were producing something that everyone would need someday, was the distance for traditional work models in favor of different means of interpreting what they were building for the future. Thus, they started to use new technologies to develop products that would become essential to all of society in a near future, based upon cumulated functional knowledge.

To many people, success and peace are situations programmed for a likely future, in a standard work model, defining and practicing with discipline and organization. To others, the desired future can be created in countless manners, even randomly, as there are so many variables interrelated that an unexpected movement can cause the disturbance of many, deeply altering the expected results and desirable goals. If for the acts and external facts, determining for future projects, there are no defined, specific core, then the only consistent condition for the success are the variables who can be manually manipulated, and that can limit, difficult or help the construction of actions and routines to achieve a goal.

Undoubtedly, huge amounts of knowledge, control and effort are crucial for the effective, relatively efficient conclusion of any idealized project. However, to fail, quit or lose, it is enough to assure the overlooking of a few controllable actions and fundamental attitudes, and wait for the failure to become real and unavoidable.

Among many conditions that lead to the failure of projects, certainly the greatest of them, is to act without a defined schedule or without a basic schematization. If there is something that can start already as an expected failure is action by impulse, and without programming, without definition of stages, processes, materials, people or simply the absence of the minimum organizational conditions for its implementation in a determined period.

Unfortunately, many projects start without the necessary implementation schedule. Acting based on improvisation and producing at any cost, or to "go with the flow", and when failure approaches, leaving only a single possibility, which is to give up and try to start again, and always with a book of nonsensical apologies.

Any project who intends to develop entirely needs a basic pipeline, which defines at least why, when, how, whom and what is available during the operation. Many projects, even though following this basic scheme, are not performed on the right time, or even not performed at all when lacking a direction. Nevertheless, people or teams who can answer satisfyingly these issues are more likely to thrive.

Another important condition to failing, in any situation, is the lack of focus, the light that guides the long road all to way until fulfilling the goal. Focus is fundamental always. If planning indicates how to achieve the goal efficiently, focus is the horizon where we must arrive and must be seen as the project's main objective, and straying from it means to abandon the initial project and to drifting in darkness and uncertainty.

Companies and professionals focused in developing the future do not change focus when the external conditions change, as they change continuously. If every change in external conditions alter the purpose of the project, then the result will be many unanswered questions without conclusion, battering the soul and losing time.

Another important issue to assure failure is to insist in doing everything on your own, which is virtually impossible for human being always lived in groups and are highly cooperative social animals, who can only fulfill themselves in society.

To act alone stresses the basic difficulties of every action. Increases work time, diminishes the study time, vanquishes the reflection time and feedbacks and, lastly, limits specialization the greatest differential in modern humankind's cooperative organization. Not even God did it all alone, according to the sacred texts of Christian tradition, in Genesis 1:26, "Let us make mankind in our image, in our likeness"[2]. Literally, the text points out that God should have had some assistants, required to help him in the difficult idea of creating a human being from the intertwining of countless body cells, organs and tissues, and even a soul.

To know how to share ideas and results, to be able to lead collective objectives and to deal with constructive adversities are the essential conditions to avoid failure, as the sum of the parts is always something else than the whole, something way beyond each collaborator's individual contribution. Sharing work enables specialization, through the division of tasks among the group, tending to grant more efficiency to the working processes and management operation.

Yet, to fail, in both business and life, it is to give up the planned objective when the first complications arrive. Any professional, conscious of what trying to build, knows perfectly that they must focus and persevere even when it seems to fall apart. They even realize, eloquently, that mistakes and failures are learning instead of incentive to accepting the loss.

The word "persist" comes from two Latin terms: *"per"*, which means "through", and *"sistere"*, which means "to stand", agglutinated into the word "persistere", in a sense of standing firmly through, even when conditions change and everything seems to be over because of some difficulty. To persist is important when knowing how far it can go and how. Persistence is fundamental in conducting any project, and sometimes constitutes in the main asset for the aimed success.

Nowadays, the modern work environment assemble different tasks, isolate or intertwined, from the lecture of e-mails to analyzing financial risks, daily updated. In this scenario, there any many ways of classifying the tasks, which can come from the simpler to the more complex, from the more urgent to the supplementary, or yet from the profitable to the damaging.

In this aspect, depending on the values and the routine the team or the company sustains, I believe the simpler could be done first. This assertion is a little different from what some theorists believe. By I do believe that to perform the less time-demanding tasks after everything else to be a crucial point to not concluding tasks, and thus, disappointment and failure.

I worked in a company where my manager cumulated piles of tasks, from different client requirements the Bank had interest in conducting business with, where the priority where from the more urgent, or the more complex, to the quick solving, less complex problems.

When he left in vacations, he also left his countless piles of work for me to "manage". First, I classified each of the papers in complexity order, from the simpler, which proved to be around 80% of the piles, to the more complex. Then, I started to work first on the simpler processes, whose conclusion was quicker, took less time and made the work more productive. In two weeks, I have solved 90% of the tasks he left cumulating for months.

When the manager came back from his vacation, he could not believe in my efficiency and proposed himself to reanalyze those tasks I have worked on and he concluded that its conclusion was, indeed, conclusive. The remaining tasks could be calmly analyzed, because they were fewer and required a higher level of care, without the stress, pressure and discouragement of an unsolvable pile of paperwork.

Another important point to those who aim to fail or go bankrupt, which I would like to share particularly, consists in persisting in not sharing mistakes, believing that the others and the world, and to make mistakes alone is better and nobler. This frivolous attitude constitutes in a trait of professionals who will not thrive for long or companies that will soon vanish. Mistakes have always been part of the human progress, and we will never get rid of it. To err is healthy when trying to build something bigger, and when knowing you took the wrong path. As Pe. Zezinho, Brazilian priest and musician, used to claim in his famous song "The falls I have had were not defeats. I fell when trying to climb. And to climb means to want to be in a state above the one you were before".

When sharing mistakes, we divide the responsibilities, we sum the efforts, we accept difficulties and we teach others how to not proceed, making a personal error become a social knowledge, besides the feedback we can internalize when relegating to the others the conditions and consequences of failures inherent to the process. It is a huge mistake to not learn with our mistakes, neither with the mistakes shared by the others.

Finally, to live in a continuously moving world and permanent transformation requires a routine of constant reading and interpretation as learning is an important part of work itself[3], modifying as we modify it ourselves. Those who eventually cannot get familiar to the practice of reading do not possess many assets an enterprise can use, and cannot build alternative technical structures when the great paradigmatic changes come.

The practice of reading strengthens the mind, flowers ideas and stimulates the creativity, making people with discipline to such to achieve a higher quality of life, subjective and objective, more fulfilling than the rest[4]. Without it, the individual becomes similar to an organism who, lacking the conditions to live, accepts to slowly die in an environment who managed to overwhelm it until its last breath, progressively leading it to failure as Bob Dylan famously ironized in his song "Like a Rolling Stone".

> How does it feel, how does it feel?
> To be without a home
> Like a complete unknown,
> Like a rolling stone...

The Merciless Art of Copying n' Pasting

This topic's title could simply be "copying and pasting and following the song", as most of this book is about associating famous songs to the educational and organizational processes of modernity. But, to those who lived through the sad experience of being tortured, as the singer/songwriter Geraldo Vandré, maybe it would be unflattering to the message I intend to pass on, about the professionals who work over the board on the basis of the Ctrl + C/ Ctrl + V.

The insertion of computer systems enhanced work tools in offices, homes, armies and universities, contributed to compacting spaces used to keep important files by making available smaller products frequently, and to the reduction of the production costs, and consequently the reduction of work posts. Before the e-mail and personal computer era, the more efficient and modern office equipment were the typewriters and a good copying machine. One for producing texts, and the other to reproducing them according to the company's necessity, and once read they were filed in boxes or dossiers inside huge lockers, and were open again only for consultation or alteration of its content.

Enterprises' internal communication was slow, as the process of receiving and sending written memos or mail needed to go through the hands of a good secretary, who typewrote word by word, and when finished, had to be photocopied and sent.

Personal computers text editors were a huge advance in office's technology and became indispensable for any professional in any field. One of the more "efficient" computer tools is the Ctrl + C/Ctrl + V command, who enable to copy words of a preexistent text and place them in a text currently being produced or edited.

It would be a wondrous tool if its use were not so radical, to the point where it inhibits creativity and innovation of ideas and proceedings. If on one hand it standardizes the textual production, on the other hand it collaborates to the law of the lesser effort, inherent to some professionals and that sometimes infects many departments in companies and public agencies, with the intention to impose radically a pattern.

The art of copying and pasting started between texts of a same databank, filed in a personal computer, available in a same server. Ever since sharing in terminal networks and workstations, many people granted access to the files, and this procedure thrived even more after the indiscriminate possibility of copying remote files through the internet. What began as a way to ease the burden of a copyist or a typewriter became an indiscriminate tool, surpassing the product's specifications to the point of achieving a "departmental asset" in a global scale.

As to have an idea of how ingrained in companies organization the "Ctrl +C/ctrl +V" culture is, I was looking for a job back in 2005, and went to the selection agency of a big company on the energetics' sector. After a quick interview, I was submitted, along a few other candidates, to a 40-question test, 20 about math and 20 about the Portuguese language, to be answered on the span of an hour. After finishing the exam, they informed me to wait for an eventual return for an interview with one of the company's directors, which happened in five days. Three days after this test, the HR of one of the world's biggest brands contacted me for a test, in the financial sector. Arriving on the designated location, there was 50 other people, and the first stage of our selection would be a Portuguese and Mathematics test, to be submitted on the span of one hour.

We were conducted to another room; I sat on the front row and waited for instructions about the test. When I received the test paper, for my huge surprise, it was the same test I did a few days earlier, on other company. They did not even changed the sequence of the questions nor of the alternatives.

I could not believe it to be true, and wondered how the culture of copying and pasting inserted itself even in traditional, big corporation's structures. I finished the test in five minutes, because I already knew all the answers, and when I rose up to deliver it, every other contender looked at me with sheer disbelief. Probably they wondered I was some kind genius or assumed I was just friends of someone in that company who elaborated the questions, and thus I should have known the answers in advance, for it was impossible to do all those calculations in less than forty minutes.

The answer was neither. I was simply favored by the lack of creativity and responsibility of the professionals in that recruiting department, which, instead of elaborating a specific exam, unique to the company's procedures, would rather research in a site the questions they needed to measure the level of writing and calculation of the job applicants.

It is hard to believe that, among the company's support activities, there is not a constant necessity of revision or innovation regarding the contents worked or practiced. The recurring revision of proceedings can strengthen the work process, mitigates the risks and, specially, it steers way the possibility of repeating evitable mistakes, tending to eliminate the excessive accommodation by nulling the copy/paste, present daily on the work of some lazy professionals.

The more dynamic teams and companies rarely copy, and more often tend to be copied and followed in whatever qualifies and values more their brands. It is an absurd paradox, as one of their most valued qualities is precisely the quality of their work and constant innovation.

As the company is a living organism, the composition of its individual parts are also living beings, composed by people and processes that summed up become a larger reality. As such, the deficient culture of the necessity of copying and pasting, if not fought off, discouraged and limited, will stablish itself as the dominant form of the whole organism, causing the complete operational frailty and troubling the capacity of innovating and adapting to new circumstances, and consequently leading to its death.

On the modern corporate world, standardization, or the efficient form of copy/paste, is among the company's internal procedures, and ever among the company's external contenders, acquired vainly in weak websites scattered all over the internet. Every company develops a sense of self-organization and self-knowledge, which is unique and runs accordingly to its values and technological conditions it has available for its collaborator's chains.

The efficient company in the post-modern work must standardize its processes, promoting creativity and constant innovations, similarly to what systemic vision calls dynamic balance, where the systems are in harmony, but looking for innovation after interactions with the outer systems who nourishes them. Absorbing the main qualities, but adapting them to its operational structure and the capacity of its professional ranks in following these changes in a standard, rhythmical and balanced way.

Around 200 years ago, before being mercilessly beheaded by his old enemies, Lavoisier asserted that nothing in nature is created nor lost, it is rather transformed, relating his scientific discoveries to the continuous flow of material compounds in nature. On the modern scenario, many professionals around the world are thinking against Lavoisier, as "in my department, nothing is created, nothing is lost, nothing is transformed... everything is copied, and then pasted". Unfortunately, those who assert and practice it tirelessly will soon be "beheaded" from their jobs, sooner or later.

I sincerely hope that the reader of these few pages is not one of those who will have the decapitation as the sad ending of a career or job who could otherwise be better. But may it be an intense reflection about the intellectual limitations the art of copying and pasting can ingrain on the human mind, resulting in a system of laziness, mental atrophy and lingering professional mediocrity, making that, on the mid-run, without creativity or perspective of alternatives in jobs and employment, this person feels horrified, tired and discouraged. Like the character in the famous song "Hallowed Be Thy Name", from the great English band Iron Maiden, about the reflections of someone who is about to face execution, when he sadly asserts to himself:

> Waiting in my cold cell, when the bell begins to chime
> Reflecting on my past life
> And it doesn't have much time
> (...)The sands of time for me are running low[5]

It is Difficult to Rebuild

One of the greatest philosophers in the 1600's was John Locke, who, among many other books, published in "Essay concerning human understanding" that the human mind is a white paper, and every personal knowledge would be acquired after the experience of every human being cumulated along their lives, which is partially true. Nowadays, this assertion is systematically fought off or modified, as countless researches have shown that many mental processes are independent of human consciousness, or are unconscious, besides the genetic factors that determine the formation of intelligence and individual skills, constructed after comprehension of personality.

Modern Science has progressively given new interpretations to the realities we judge as true, after the knowledge of how the cerebral process in our minds condition or determine our personality, our choices or how we understand the world, as:

By treating the issue of our identity, we are facing one of the most controversial subjects in psychology. The points of view are the most diverse and vary from the exaggerated emphasis on our innate predispositions (...), to the belittlement of this aspects, understanding that we are more than that, dependent on our cultural formation and the familiar context we were raised into.[6]

Nowadays there is a shared conviction that the mind, the consciousness, intelligence and personality are independent structures, connecting through the same mental process: the electrical impulses produced by the neurons inside the brain, whose main purpose is unclear to many. The more advanced studies in about the human mind and consciousness have been trying to demonstrate an absolute inexistence of an extracorporeal human soul, and yet have found difficulties in categorizing the "self", or the individual personality as an conscious entity, independent and autonomous who commands everyone's individual action through the free will of thoughts and actions.

Human conscience is a product of minds, there is no doubt about it, and the level of knowledge each one achieves is the product of one's own individual consciousness, or even collective, as many believe. However, personal knowledge – the one each one carries within – and social knowledge – the one each may share or learn – manifests itself in a level of conscious mental state many of us think as unique and true. There is no indication we could have a same level of knowledge or world perception in another unconscious mental state. This subject is as controversial nowadays as the general notions about personalities and conditions in which differential knowledge is effectively created.

On the other hand, many still consider, just like St. Augustine, that consciousness is an exclusive gift from God to men, whose main goal is to acquire intellectual abilities to glorify His name and conscience and personality are only manifestations of the same divine essence. Nonetheless, without any intention of value upon such claims and considering only issues regarding the conscious knowledge we acquire and try to pass on to our peers, certainly that by living or inhabiting the world, individuals cumulate and share implied knowledge about what surrounds them, a social product generated by the intimate interaction between people.[7] The cultural environment where one lives and grows is determining for his intellectual formation, if not in total, at least a significant amount.

The mind can live independently of the consciousness, which can be only a product for the latter's amusement or hobby. Our personality may as well not be entirely ours, as we believed for thousands of years. However, for sure, the knowledge we acquire by any means belongs to the conscious mind, which we feed and carry until the end of our life, or conscience itself, and one of the essential jobs of the knowledge process is to assure the acquisition of new skills to be used to grant a better level of existence.

In this sea of doubt, many researches were aimed at trying to comprehend the integrated knowledge of brain, mind, conscience and how it interrelates to form what we understand as "self". However, many of these researches were conducted with the goal of producing tools that connected directly to people's brain, could enhance their intelligence, strength and memory in a level of knowledge above the remaining human beings.

In this same direction, in 1999 an American movie named "Gattaca"[8] came out, a story about the class struggle between the class of the superior, genetically enhanced humans and the natural, unmodified humans. Upon conception, every – wealthy – one had the opportunity to be bestowed with genetic alterations, which would improve their physical, chemical and mental performance, with the supervision of the potent modern science. After this, every opportunity to learn, work, careers and social status was given in consonance to the enhancement each individual possess, creating a closed class of super humans.

In this narrative, life experiences had little to no influence in constructing people's personality, as every condition to exist and think were determined by the genetic composition induced during gestation, which would control the development of the organism, from the cradle to the grave.

In the movie, besides the dark futuristic environment and the fraud promoted by the main character, the narrative develops around the attempts of an unimproved, natural human to equal himself to others who underwent enhancement. By enrolling himself in a school who prepares super-humans to space travelling, he tries to prove to himself that every human being, when determined in fulfilling a goal, are equally capable, with or without chemical influences or genetic improvement.

Although in a system where people underwent a genetic and biological improvement, would the human mind still be a white paper as stated by Locke? What if conscience was a more advanced, with a high degree of genetic influence, would it be the possibility of erasing negative lines and rewriting them just by annulling or reordering genes?

The answer for the first question is still yes; experiences would keep molding our conscience and could still change our personality as the years go by. However, to the second question, the most obvious at this precise moment would be no. There are not enough indications that we could erase our past by simply rewriting or reordering our genetic structure. If we are willing to talk to our conscience intimately, it would probably tell us that the more correct answer would be to take a few learnings from the losses and failures we suffer, instead of trying to delete it from memory, which would enable to reconstruct another learning that would qualify the mind to acquire new abilities and accept other possibilities of being and acting with the real genetic and biologic resources we have.

Our conscience would remain as such. What we must not admit is that occasional natural limitations became conditions to peacefully embrace defeat and failure as a perpetual condemnation, as a never changing, absolute reality. Not unlike what happened to Prometheus after aiding constantly the humans and betraying the almighty Zeus, and was condemned to live chained to a same reality forever or until redemption, being hurt by a flail who would hack a piece of his liver daily.

Many financial resources are invested in researches to develop mechanisms that can improve genetically the skills of humans who can afford it. But the results of this induced genetic improvements may not be as impressing as the scientists wish it to be, for the manipulation of an expensive and complex technology. Besides being able to create additional motivation to those who consider the natural human being unbeatable in form, beauty and intelligence, which would allow the countless chained Prometheus to start trying by themselves to leave the prison imposed to them, by acquiring new knowledge and new skills.

The improvement of many human capacities induced by genetic manipulation, just like the myth of Prometheus, further away in time as they may seem, still reflects some situations in modern days. It can relate especially to the professionals who avoid learning new skills, and chain their bodies and souls to the high ends of fictional mountains, protected or imposed by the mighty Zeus of modern era, the veteran occupants of the higher ranks in the company. Having to endure daily the pains caused by stress or pressure for not being able to produce, innovate or create more, to live better in a cooperative environment, or even to having to answer for mistakes daily, until the unavoidable demission or compulsory retirement, when not even a mental breakdown.

Yet, many professionals who live in discouragement on their work spaces waiting for a divine or genetic miracle spend too much of their time and energy hoping that conditions change, than properly trying to create the conditions to their self-improvement along the time.

Machiavelli said that the human tragedy is that circumstances change, men do not. In an environment where changes are extreme, to remain steady atop your former self or waiting for the help of god becomes a huge competitive disadvantage on the labor's market, because sometimes our former self, who may not even exist any longer, was constructed in wondrous sceneries along time, and only remained alive in memories and old preserved photos. But we cannot invite it out often to grab a beer, listen to some good music and ask it to help us to keep moving. We can only have it as an example of what we have been through, what we learned and have not succeeded. And as we will never be able to delete it from ourselves, not even by inducing chemicals or genetic manipulation, as some typo in a text, our experiences can indicate that one of the main conditions in life is precisely the continuous change, progressively, and that our mistakes are only a matter of opinion.

To change, in a broader sense, would not only leaving Catholicism and adopting Presbyterianism, and after that Protestantism, as often seen around. Chang is not implanting microchips, either. It means to rebuild steadily, in function of the dynamic conditions that the environment stablishes. To change is to go new paths we want to know, growing up with them and realizing that life is something we have to build every day. The pace does not matter, only the conscience that standing still, always looking back, will turn a human being into a sand statue which the wind will blow quickly and merciless, as Bob Dylan once wrote:

> And admit that the waters
> Around you have grown
> And accept it that soon
> You'll be drenched to the bone.
> If your time to you
> Is worth savin'
> Then you better start swimmin'
> Or you'll sink like a stone
> For the times they are a-changin'.[9]

To rewrite oneself is not yet possible. To acquire new skills via genetic manipulation, neither. So, the adequate, human solution to keep growing is to reinvent ourselves, or reinterpret after the structures that continuously form as the time passes have the same form that the human mind develop to construct our conscience. We should seek to always acquire new abilities, and learn to handle properly the new tools that make the processes more efficient and practical, absorbing new ideas, new formulas and new considerations about the fundamental traits of human existence itself, making the human being more prepared to endure mistakes of the time and the solutions of the present. Deep down, it is all that matters to follow with our heads up, and trying to overcome everyday more, as we cannot live forever "trying to try", nor deleting the mistakes and disappointments of live.

It is Important not to be Insitutionalized

One of the best movies I have ever watched, which made me cry for hours unending, was "The Shawshank Redemption".[10] The American movie, written and directed by Frank Darabont, stars Tim Robbins and Morgan Freeman or their best roles. In my humble opinion, the director managed to brightly construct the film around a complex interpretation context, composed by many traits who develop far beyond the main plot, the permanent prison break and the retook of freedom of the Andy Dufresne (Tim Robbins), inmate who claims to be innocent.

Despite every difficulty and having to endure the loss of freedom and the abrupt change in life after penal seclusion, especially when pleading innocence, the movie portrays quite sophisticatedly the network of relationships, dependence and friendships build inside the prisons, as to replicate in that environment a few essential situations to pacific coexistence of the outside world. Although faced with disbelief and disqualification by society, the inmates make an effort, on their way, to construct and enable relationships of trust, respect and mutual support among their peers, partners or those upon who they exercise some sort of power, as the prison is the only place where power can manifest itself in a pure state, in its more excessive dimension and justify itself as moral power.[11]

In one of the movie's more intriguing scenes, Ellis "Red", Freeman's character, commenting on the suicide of a former-inmate, who was friends with everyone and lived nearly his entire life behind bars, attributes that desperate action to the "institutionalization" who haunts people who were deprived of their freedom. Living daily with the internal rules of a strict penitentiary system, the individual can no longer relate outside it, without strict rules, without daily orders, without the counting and, above all, without the circle of friends with whom he lived through his years in prison, who were no longer around to share stories nor difficulties of everyday life.

Leaving prison after some long years, the former-inmate feels the same hardships he felt on his first days inside jail, but in a more acute manner, as the world he once known in freedom fell behind. His more intimate relationships remained in prison or lost in time, as the best years of the life he could have lived.

Red asserts that institutionalization refers to the essential traits an inmate – and people, generally – assume after years living in the same reality, inside or outside prison and with time becomes the only way to exist, in a different world apart from the rest. He claims that people institutionalized in a certain condition, as in prison for a long time, cannot live, produce, create or relate in different environments. They must live restricting themselves to certain conditions and behaviors, which configured their lifestyle for long periods.

Ever since birth, every human being goes through a process of education, socialization and circumstantial institutionalization, which will determine how each person lives accordingly to their conditions and existential limitations of the environment they live and share. The social structures like religion, school, government and community will induce behavioral patterns according to the collective world perception these structures believe to be true, imposing to the rest of the group their specific values, beliefs and philosophy. In this aspect, it is harder to develop behaviors and even ideas different from whatever the so-called "system" imposes to its "participants". For instance, nobody expects that a white, Christian Brazilian would wish to study to develop the spiritual skills necessary to being a shaman to the Mura tribe, in the middle of the Amazon, which would go against the basic standard model of his Christian belief. Nonetheless, nobody expects a Dessana shaman to want to become a bishop in the Universal Church in Manaus, and teaches Christianity to his tribal peers.

Among this huge structuring system, there are subsystems that condition even more how people act and think. Particularly, these subsystems are responsible for institutionalizing people to behave similarly to their closest ones, but differently of the standard total. For instance, to the white Christians, it is common belief that Jesus Christ is the Son of God, and that one day he will come to save us from eternal damnation. However, it is hard for a catholic citizen to believe that Saturday is the day of rest determined by God, as claimed by the

Seventh-Day Adventists. This is a textbook example of how a totalizing system can be more specific inside the macro systems that institutionalizes people through religion.

Thus, people institutionalized in the smaller structuring systems tend to feel difficulty integrating or interacting outside the subsystem, which imposes more restrictions and determined their cultural formation, as well as their relevant professional qualifications. In the modern world, unfortunately, many institutions and companies count among their ranks professionals institutionalized on their own internal environments. It is deeply concerning, especially to the professionals who tend to be unable to understand circumstances usual to a wider reality, outside of their limited, restricting work environment, who do not yet propose themselves to search for a wider meaning to their own purposes.

I worked in a bank institution where I could hear daily from employees who had spent more than 20 years in the company that, if they left it, they would not be able to do much outside, for everything they knew how to perform was according to the institution's procedures. The great problem to everyone was precisely this, the company was looking for a way to fire them as soon as possible, as the professional competences required for the banking career had changed, and many of those older employees fell behind regarding the qualifications the institution needed.

Nowadays, in any economic sector company, it is possible to perceive that what the employees want and seek to develop for their lives and careers, and what the organizations need or offer, are often in conflict or do not fit properly, and in these situations, the necessity of the company tends to prevail, always. Thus, the professional, highly centered in his career, must be aware that whenever the company no longer needs its services, he will be unconditionally fired. Independent of moral, ethical or existential considerations. As such, this professional must seek to grow, expand and make possible that when the company no longer fits his/hers purposes and ambitions properly, he or she can remorselessly cast it away.

The more focused professionals seek to continuously acquire new knowledges to develop their skills, which can provide an elevated differential regarding their contenders for the best available work posts.

Most companies tend to force their employees to integrate themselves to the work process efficiently, and afterwards they will build their careers. However, it does not impedes people of having the extraordinary sense of understanding where careers and qualifications are heading. Integrating efficiently to the company's process, but developing competences who can adequate to any company and process or institutional environment outside it.

Getting rid of organizational institutionalization is one of the most efficient ways of putting oneself ahead of the essential conditions that will define jobs and careers, besides projecting the mind to pursing other things in life who are really worth it. Still, being able to enrich the mind with safer skills to think and build new things, besides being able to continuously acquire knowledge to perfect the performance and constructive attitudes in any career.

If the mind is really the essence of being alive, it is much likely there is no other form of existence outside and beyond it, for it is on the mind that the true substance of life thrives, the human consciousness, which is unique and individual, and can project to countless possibilities of existence from our choices and attitudes. Even if there is a huge world trying to condition our existence, to know how to choose whatever makes us happy is always the best. The worst form of existence is precisely when our choices are put against our conscience, forcing us to live according to what is possible, sadly condition to an institutionalization that is worse than prison, and that slowly excludes the individual from itself, its dreams and the plentitude that life can offer. When we can be ourselves, controlling our lives and adjusting what cannot be controlled, including our dreams, as in the amazing song "Silent Lucidity", by the American group Queensrÿche, released in the 1990's album "Empire":

> If you open your mind for me
> You won't rely on open eyes to see
> The walls you built within
> Come tumbling down, and a new world will begin
> Living twice at once you learn
> You're safe from pain in the dream domain
> A soul set free to fly
> A round trip journey in your head
> Master of illusion, can you realize
> Your dream's alive, you can be the guide

The Greatest Heritage is the Cultural One

I was with my daughter, passing in front of a school when I stopped behind an imported muscle car, whose owner left a student in that institution. Seeing this, my daughter why didn't we buy a car like that. I answered that if I bought that kind of car, I would not have enough resources to pay for her school, and I would have to enroll her in that same school we were passing by, which was not that good for the career she was intending to follow, and cars are disposable, but knowledge is not.

In another situation, I was taking my fiancée's father home, after spending a few days with us. I parked just outside his house, and opening up the door of my car for him to leave, it briefly touched another vehicle, which was parked there too. Quickly, the owner came deeply infuriated, and ordered me to move my car. I said I would not, because my father-in-law had locomotion issues* and I would only leave when I could take him safely out of the car and into his house, obviously. This fact provoked an extremely frustrated attitude on that citizen, who could not perceive anything beyond the limit of his ego, as he did not even volunteered his help.

What these two anecdotes have in common is the fact that it becomes clearer that people tend to value inanimate objects over other people. And many of the undervalued people are usually our children, wives, fathers, mothers, and other people we should love and cherish above all.

Life is infinite, but we, sadly, have an expiration date, and we are always leaving things behind, for the future or oblivion. In the end, we are obliged to leave for good the world we know and helped to build, leaving only parts of our genetic, moral, economic and cultural inheritance.

During many centuries of human history, the only inheritance parents could leave to their children was the biological, often product of rape, debts, kidnapping or alcohol abuse. Countless people born, lived and died without knowing their biological fathers. Only after the advances of monogamist wedding, a manner of granting lawful legitimacy to the heirs ant the transfer of the father's patrimony to his children, was when people finally acknowledge and valued the fatherhood and the material wealth of the patriarch, as his name and social entitlement. Many theorists claim it was the main socially relevant reason to have monogamist weddings on the first place, during Antiquity: to assure the birthright to the inheritance to those who really carried the father's genes, which was hard to determine before having knowledge of human genetic structure.

After consolidating monogamist wedding and the constitution of family through the father's optics, the main inheritance left to their children, which were before inexistent, now was purely economic, constituted by estates, money, slaves, animals, concubines and land. The wedding's main function was to raise children whose paternity is undisputed, for they will come into their father's property as his natural heirs.[12]

For countless years, marriage had nothing but an economic motivation, especially regarding the most powerful families, who saw it as the possibility of a less dangerous union to increase wealth, lands, power and prestige between friends and foes alike.

In the modern world, where paternity can be assured by biologic science, the heirs can acquire goods through legal mandatory decrees, owning land is longer the main source of wealth, monogamist wedding lost most of its initial value and long lasting weddings are not as important as they used to be. In a world where nothing is made to last[13], the affective and matrimonial relationships are less and less effective. Some people even think about it as a financial liability and a drawback in the professional career. Although the monogamist wedding no longer represents the life goal of many modern men and women, the same cannot be said about children, who still largely desired by couples around the world, especially by homosexual couples.

Thus, considering that children are more important than wedding and knowledge became the greatest asset to generating wealth and a major differential in any business or career, we can assure that the greatest inheritance these parents can legate to their children is the cultural heritage, undoubtedly. The level of knowledge, discipline to acquire more knowledge and relevant values when passed onto children will enable them to know the world safely and with conviction, and to know themselves solidly, producing the fundamental basis to what they can achieve, build, possess or transform along their lives when they became independent adults.

Jobs and careers, friends and everything else one day will be over, for one reason or another. Then, we have to start over a new routine, afar from the things we lived with and from whatever we got used to, when the children already display their own routines and start to deal with their own problems, when friends are no longer around and the body starts warn it may want to rest – forever. When this moment comes, we should be happy if the cultural heritage we legated to our descendants is a result of love, care and trust we forged in those who will continue to live life when we are swallowed by the merciless ritual of death. And this is priceless. Nothing could pay off more than the pride and happiness of seeing a defenseless child become a productive, responsible, trustworthy citizen, as motivated as their parents taught.

Nowadays, there are many problems regarding personality and behavioral formation of youngsters, who find a reason for their existential problems in their parents, who lack in love, care or in listening properly. Many parents occupy themselves in assuring the largest possible economical heritage, leaving little space for affective or cultural issues, only realizing this mistake when their children lose their control on the abuse of alcohol, drugs or crime. The modern world indeed produced generations of children estranged from their parents, who rarely could meet with them during the day to talk or have lunch, s most of the necessary care was outsourced to kindergartens, churches or schools. As a result, the cultural formation of many children is completely different, if not divergent from their parents', which in a way enforced the construction of more and more complicated and empty relationships between parents and children, who would rather trust barely-known individuals in remote social network than the barely-known individuals in their own home.

Yet, many parents believe their children are their belongings to manage after their convictions and frustrations, in a completely different world from the one where these convictions were formed or made sense. We have to understand that our kids are not our property, and we should let them free to live a life who is theirs only, and no one else's. The cultural heritage we must transmit is the one who is determining to the intellectual, moral and professional formation that can show the ways to the spiritual search they want for themselves. Never what we want to see on the others more deeply than what we seek to ourselves. This is fundamental.

The cultural heritage we intend to transmit to our descendants must be considered in the systemic vision of life phenomena's conception. In other words, it should account not only the particular patriarchal culture, but also fundamentally the values who guide the values of the family itself, where both parents share an affective, healthy relationship, determining in the constitution of the heirs' personalities.

Many parents insist in their children following their previous steps, inhibiting creativity, impeding a path that could be more fulfilling to those who follow it apart from their parents and trusting in themselves. To make it worse, there are parents who invest more time and resources on their own hobbies than on the quality of their children's education, which will be their most valuable good on the formation and professional career. In doing so, they deprive their children from the appropriation of a knowledge level proper for achieving a higher professional ground and regardless the fact that *the demand for moderately skilled workers declined as repetitive jobs were gradually displaced by computer programs.*[14]

The concern with the children's formation is so relevant that the national states have been approving punitive laws against parent's who neglect it, a crime known as intellectual abandon, typified as the parent's failure in granting the enrollment in an educational institution and the lack of concern in accompanying the education of their children. In Brazil, this crime is profiled in the art. 246 of the Penal Code. However, due to the inefficiency of the scholar dynamics, there is yet to be created a reasonable structure to punish the parents responsible for this crime.

Regardless the attempts to criminalize the lack of interest of parents in their children's education, the cultural and educational incentive we should provide is largely supplied by the Information Era, which contributed to the agility, efficiency and dynamics of the qualified work. On the other hand, it has had devastating consequences to less qualified workers, leaving them apt only for underemployment situations or eventual freelances, or even begging for a living. This process can become even crueler in the future labor market, where many people born or raised right now will lack completely the conditions to attain a formal job, because of their lack of qualifications and skills that the enterprises may need.

Without any further ado, the investment in culture and knowledge basis that can be shared with the children are the best gift we can leave to them. When they receive this gift, they may have conditions to build a more fulfilling life, a more solid career and a cleaner, healthier life, besides one day being able to pass on what they learned from their parents and more. We must always think that we work hard everyday for our kids only, trying to construct a better world, without the necessity to caging and limiting them as in the Pink Floyd's song, "Mother", where

> Mama's gonna keep you right here under her wing.
> She won't let you fly, but she might let you sing.
> Mama's gonna keep baby cozy and warm.
>
> ... and imprisoned in his own world.

***My father in law is a wheelchair user.**

The World of Limitless Information

The French sociologist Jean Baudrillard claims that we live in a world where there is more and more information, and less and less meaning[15], as to describe this situation where information floods our e-mails, televisions and smartphones all the time. However, it only means that most people consume so much information that they can no longer develop an accurate sense of reading, which could be an asset to make them more efficient and apt to work in enterprises and governments.

The modern world most remarkable trait is the production of high level and high-speed information, where part of society structure itself to make a living out of the production, circulation and accumulation of information that can be shared, transformed into knowledge and monetized through countless chains of processes and absorption of rotating content, as never seen before.

For thousands of years, the transmission of knowledge and teaching of the youngest has been through the orality, where the eldest shared their group's creeds and expertise during socialization. This form of learning was essential for the availability of the facts and myths of the man and women from the past to the future generations, and is one of the most touchingly beautiful of life narration for those who saw and heard it as a way to find themselves in the world and interpret it.

Oral knowledge transmission remained alive for many generations, even after the advances of the writing systems. The main difference between the oral transmission of the old societies and the mass transmission of media common in the contemporary world is that in antiquity the facts were accepted as universal truths. Where the tales told and sung was the supreme knowledge about life and organization of tribes and families, who developed their systems since the truths they received from the elders, from generation to generation. Contrarily, nowadays it is fundamental to pose question marks in the information received daily, as many cloak themselves in political, personal, ideological and even fake considerations, for countless reasons.

Many theorists agree that in the modern age, knowledge is nothing but the ability to filter information, who circle around the world faster, enhanced by the globalization and the connection of different countries and people who share common ideas. In this aspect, the important thing is not the quantity of information we can internalize, but the quality of what we can absorb, distinguishing what is useful and how it is applicable on the search for solving problems or issues shared by people, governments and enterprises around the globe.

For Nonaka and Takeuchi, every information possess a syntactical and a semantical aspect, being the latter more important for the generation of knowledge as "information is a flow of message, while knowledge is created by the same flow of information, anchored on the beliefs and compromise of its bearer". [16] This flow of message has become so intense to the point where we need constantly the help of more powerful computers to process the huge amount of information we receive daily.

Another important issue is that nowadays, in the constitutional democracies, beside many people who do not care for fact checking, it is easier to have a specific, unique and particular opinion about the relevant matters, which was not possible in the old societies, where the opinion of the official positions of kings, prophets, wises and saints was irreproachable. This contributed to the fact that ancient societies were able to remain apparently stable for long generations, since the processing of information was restricted and specific, besides the immense difficulty of mass sharing of this scarcely produced information. It is reasonably difficult to imagine that, after thousands of years, one might disagree that all humans came from the divine breath or blood placed in a clay body molded by a creator god, or that the falling rain was natural for the cycle of water, because whoever did it would most likely be severely punished.

Many also claim that in modern days, people possess too much information and too little knowledge. Considering that knowledge is a flow of information consolidated in a broader dimension and that, despite the existence of a large array of methods to circle information instantaneously, most people cannot relate the information they receive to the application in situations that require more personal skills. Besides, the infinite and uncontrollable flow of information quite often does not find a hold in truth or reality.

Many studies have sought to demonstrate that a vast majority of information circulating around the world is false, fanciful or invented with some purpose. It became such a big issue that technology companies, in partnership with universities, created a fund to counter the fake information that floods the internet. Yet, among so many denominations given to today's world as post-industrial, post-patriarchal, post-Christian, post-mechanic and postmodern, it has also been called the post-truth world. Among the false information, we can cite that Brazil handed the World Cup by a millionaire agreement with Germany in 2014, just as it did with France in an earlier Cup. Nevertheless, those who are passionate about and follow football on several level knew that Brazil was not a favorite and did not have superior conditions to win those two teams neither of the times.

Another quite relevant consideration is that many people unfortunately cannot stablish interdisciplinary connections between the (true) information they receive and the conclusions they can infer from it. Besides, to many people, the internalization of facts must meet certain conditions, coated by their inner morals or values, as *the ability to transform information in knowledge requires, above all, criteria in the selection and choice, as knowledge is not cumulative, but selective.* [17] The information that can be added to each one are tools who allow to raise the level of knowledge when internalized in a systematic, organized manner, conditioned to a certain knowledge previously available, besides the essential ability to perceive the variables relevant to the knowledge intended to produce.

The large-scale production of false information was due to the very development of communication systems and the expansion of channels that produce and convey mass information, which have expanded immensely in the last decades. It allowed, among other things, the partial monopoly of information and "truths", previously centralized in the conventional means of transmitting news - radio and TV - also allowing a greater democratization on the control of the information circulating at high speed around the planet. In the decade of 1970, Toffler asserted that one of the modernity traits he coined under the term "the third wave" was precisely the demassification of the mass-communication means[18], which would enable a system of creation and circulation of information in large scale, whose sources would be unknown or ignored, through infinite networks of particular connections.

Considering that many people do not have the habit of reading and sincerely interpreting, the perverted minds have fun producing cyber trash every day, anyhow, enhanced by the speed between the time news and information circle and the idle time of their consumers. In real time, online, they produce an infinity of information channels, which troubles the fact checking and hinders the process of identifying the people responsible in order to pose penal sanctions to those who spread hate crimes, racism and support terrorism.

As such, because of the intense whirlwind formed by the increasing flow of information produced in a global scale, the quality of information became a major concern, highly important to those who need to be aware of data, facts and events essential to making accurate decisions, or yet fundamental to enabling trusting scenarios who diminishes the risks and uncertainties. It is deeply important for any professional to have the capacity of filtering information and transforming it into knowledge and competitive assets.

Thus, one of the main assets of the knowledge society professionals is to absorb the necessary information to enhance their technical level, to assure a high level of accuracy in tough decisions and the best stance regarding risk analysis, besides sharing experiences and processes in a larger flow that can become institutional knowledge.

Numbers and data do not mean nothing if not relating to a specific set of complementary information about the specific product. As it is said, a half-full glass is also a half-empty glass, and the technical value of the glass depends on the vision (or illusion) someone inputs to it.

The greatest differential that distinguishes high level professionals is precisely the fact that they can correctly use information, data and numbers seemingly disconnect, that when reunited with the same purpose, tend to enable a better professional position to those who can decode them and objectively tie them to the possibilities and events of the real world, mitigating uncertainties, limiting insecurity and granting fluidity to the systems that organize the flow of organizations.

As most of what composes the life of humankind in complex societies, the utilization of tools and the appropriation of knowledge is highly differential, as people, professionals and enterprises benefit differently from crises, from globalization, from other's mistakes and especially from the information that surrounds us every day.

Most citizens and well-informed companies who have easy access to important information systems or advanced reading cannot produce any value with the information they have, and could be used in favor of the construction of a higher-level knowledge and its application. During all of the human history, the information, as well as knowledge, where always tools of power by those who knew how to use it on their behalf, in reason of the possibilities that could be created or enhanced.

Turning Information Into Knowledge

As aforementioned, many agree that in the modern world there is an absurd flow of circling information, that cannot be internalized nor turn into productive knowledge by people, governments and enterprises. It should be considered, yet, that much of the information circling around the globe is astonishingly useless, aimed at filling some sort of emptiness that lingers on the head of many badly informed or ill-intentioned people. However, well-based and structured information can allow the construction of an essential level of knowledge to operate an array of processes in nearly every area of human existence, especially when valued, transmitted and build by public institutions and enterprises.

It should yet be considered that information and knowledge acquired a vital importance to the functioning of the post-capitalist industrial system of production, as much as the transformations introduced to the global society, particularly those regarding work, consume and interpersonal relationships.

Information and knowledge quickly became tools of high accuracy whose economic value is priceless. When applied to other processes in order to enhance efficiency as much as when only acquired in a selective manner to be later applied in knowledge generating systems that can aid people, governments and enterprises to know themselves better than they think they do, in order to stablish themselves firmly in time and space.

A few years ago, I managed a hugely problematic customer service public department, where the interactions between employees, collaborators and citizens resulted in daily conflicts. It was such a stressful environment that it reflected upon the routine of absences of a few employees, due to health issues developed in contact with that sick work place, as well as the awful quality of competence distribution and practiced routines.

In any environment, when the conflict situations and negative relationships stresses out, the solutions get tougher, because one side overlooks the demands of the other, creating a barrier impossible to overcome between the parts and imposing a destructive relationship to anyone who participates in the process, where the unconditional abandon of the respectful treatment is the only solution.

I clearly remember the first day I went there in order to diagnose what could be done in organizational improvement terms. A few hours after lunch, I sat upon an empty desk, watching the environment and reflecting about the dynamics of the customer service, when a lady came over, after somebody told her I was in charge.

First, the lady undermine me completely, because, according to her, it was unacceptable that a boss in any company or institution sits upon desks. That it was inelegant for a manager who had any sense whatsoever. After an array of "cheerful" critics, I asked what she came for, and how long she waited for the service. She informed that although arriving 10 AM, she had not yet been called, and that was the reason she resolved to ask for the sector responsible, who, for her surprise, was a man who sat upon desks. I looked at her and asked "Madam, you are waiting for about five hours and the only problem you perceived here was that the boss sits upon desks?" What a waste of purpose. Normal people in environments untainted by mutual hatred and constructed based on codependent relationships would see this scenario in a different perspective. Especially because nowadays, nobody can dispose of five hours of their precious time trying to solve an issue that could be done in five minutes, or even outside of the oppressing, sickly physical environment of the public buildings scattered across chaotic cities.

In that moment I started to realize that there were way more problems than I initially expected, and finding solutions was a matter of honor, dedication and strength. The people, though, were so deeply involved in that conflict situation that they could only point out everybody else's mistakes instead of searching for collective solutions that could enable the construction of a healthy, efficient environment, in shared process of continuous solutions, as in any living organism.

In that case, the main manager saw that the greatest problem in the department was the average waiting time was nearly about three hours, although the time envisioned by the institution should around 20 minutes. Besides the constant well based complaints by several people and organized sectors in society. From my point of view, though, the greatest problem that should be immediately fought was the stress, by annulling the conflict between the public and the employees, and raise the group's morale, which would clearly increase the service's standard and result in the lower of the average wait time, in a scheduled and coherent manner.

After that, obviously, we should bring into the service the complaints of the citizens and modern technological tools, which would enhance the efficient flow of work process and the interaction between the greater needs and real solutions. Such tools were already existent in the institution, although they were not available for the remote use of the parts interested, the citizens.

Many times, in any company, the problem is actually the result of actions or omissions that hinder the workflow, limit the creativity and demotivate the professionals into being more productive. Then, the solutions cannot happen because the true cause of the problem is never fought, nor even perceived as it should. Inefficiency is assumed to come from an unknown situation, or from the others' faults.

When the Superintendent asked me to manage that department, although everyone rose up against it, I accepted because I knew there was an efficient solution; I just did not know how, yet. I decided to read, research and gather information with other people about the issue. Most of the solutions to the daily problems began by searching information that can increase the level of expertise, as information is nearly always extensive and can be turned into concrete knowledge.

In this short period, I searched deeply about a system designed to condition the services to a pre-scheduled appointment through the internet, and saw it as a part of the solution to the department's problems, as it could enable the control of the workflow upon service offering, instead of effective demand or the screams of who cried louder.

I did a data survey about the services, systems, work process, demands and work profile of the employees. In possession of such data, I sought after a few colleagues who could add to the construction of the required solutions. We worked organizing the structure that would be essential to implement the project, considering as one of the main goals the scheduling of services that are possible to conclude and the transfer of parts of the process to remote service support, which the citizens desired the most.

The next step was to convince the employees and other collaborators that it could work and it would be much more productive to work with a relative scheduling of non-urgent services, tending to decrease the stress caused by the uncertainty regarding the working hours and the public. Besides, the worker would know in advance what the institution would like him to do each and every day.

In the first month, the waiting time decreased from nearly three hours to fifty minutes, with only about 30% of the services being scheduled. On the second month, the time decreased to twenty, and from the third on, to only fifteen minutes. It caused astonishment on many people in that institution who worked to solve many similar problems, as many of the citizens who started to see the service scheduling as beneficial to their demands.

Ever since, we receive daily mails from colleagues in other parts of Brazil who sought information about this process, and gradually this service spread across the states of the federation. In addition, it reached the customer service of countless companies and public departments, whose scheduling became central by enabling the reduction of costs, stress and external negative feedback, facing the possibility of the citizen or client scheduling when and where he will seek the service.

After managing to solve part of the problem, we decided to try to tackle the most sensitive part of the process: the need to make information available via remote interaction networks, which would surely produce an immense level of satisfaction for citizens and would earn an unimaginable scale of profit for the institution. Information should go after people, instead of the contrary. Obviously, we were not the only ones concerned about it, but we were certainly one of the first to register the institution's need to provide well-based remote access to the citizens' fiscal information.

I remember the first time I wrote to someone about the necessity of proving the taxpayers' fiscal information via internet, to what I received the reply: We will never enable this information through the internet. The second time I wrote about the same subject, I received a slightly different reply: Write this down and handle me the file. The last time, I received a different message: Congratulation, you finally did it, it is now available. To which I humbly replied "thanks, but it comes ten years late".

Technically analyzing, the most important thing we can assert, because it was fundamental for the process of change and work improvement, is that summing up seemingly disconnected and unimportant information, it was possible to create a knowledge applicable to specific problem, granting the efficiency to the service and management's dynamics. It proved to be hugely viable and useful in similar situations, who became staple to the public services all over Brazil, besides the enhancement of the internet usage as a powerful work tool, essential for the taxpayer citizen to interact with the tributary management agency.

Yet, the quality of the analyzed information was reasonably technical and free for anyone to gather, sufficing a few adjustments to make it viable to use in our general purpose. Ever since, it enabled the addition of new information to improve the work process, becoming a reference to the institution and quite relevant to society.

After the implementation of this process, we participate on a forum about costumer service along other public institutions. In this forum, we were asked about the service provided only by schedules to some services aimed at private companies, which some entities did not approve, claiming difficulty in accessing the internet, limiting the capacity of interaction with remote networks of public service offering.

At the occasion, I presented some data that placed Brazil as one of the leaders in a rank of daily access to the internet, with one of the highest percentage of time spent online. I concluded with the assertion that it that data was true, then said companies' employees would only be using the internet for leisure, instead of improving the quality of the of their work performance.

Unfortunately, the fact is that many people use the internet to absorb and distribute meaningless tasks, share useless trivia or fake news, instead of trying to take advantage of said tool to share information that adds value to their knowledge. This is not, however, a situation particular to public institutions nor private companies, but a situation present in our own houses, during the time of the Mass, on the meantime of meals, during the Christmas supper, etc. The internet is an extremely powerful tool, even for the collection, condition and processing of data useful to countless goals.

Working and Making the Imposssible

Classic literature is full of stories that could be told in a different manner, or simply updated to the modern days, considering our culture and how we write. Picture us on the condition of Noah; God descend upon earth enraged with his creation, looks you in the eyes and says: "'Sup my man, so I decided to flood the world and stuff. But as you are one faithful dude, I've decided to spare you, your family and your dog. How 'bout that?"

Impressed, you reply: "Yeah man, sure I'm happy and all, but... what do I got to do?"

God answers: "Know what? I'm tired of working for free for you guys, and to save yourself you gotta build a boat, as never seen before, using a naval technique that will only exist in like, 2000 years? And like, you have to get all by yourself, the project plus the food, clothing, all the material to take care for a real long time, cuz' earth will not dry again so soon... Oh, while you build the boat, you gotta save one couple of each animal, taking all the risks with your own resources. Sounds cool?

But hey, one more thing, just for fun would you like to lovely tell everyone on earth they're kinda screwed and they will die when the flood comes, because they suck?"

In this situation, most of us would reply as "Yeah, sure, you know, we thank you a lot for this offering but me and my family got other plans for the winter.... It's too much work, I do mostly fences and chariots. This boat thing, nah, too complicated. There is a lad down the street that works with boats, sorta... he makes rafts now and then... Pass by, see if you can close business with him. We're gonna wait for this rain and see what we can do, deal? Thanks a lot, have a nice day, My Lord."

After God leaves to go find someone else for such task, Noah goes around to grab a pint of beer and ponders with himself "Nah, that's too hard, He should do this by Himself. Dude's God, after all. Can't he just ask us the possible, bread and butter stuff? This boat thing is too much, man, I've got goats to look after, am I right?"

This is how we act and think quite often, whenever a situation seems beyond our limits and technical skills, because it is hard to imagine that the impossible can be possible through our efforts or collaboration with other people who share a common goal.

Clearly, many things are impossible due to material or technical limitations. On the other hand, few people propose themselves to construct something seemingly impossible. There is a song a consider appropriate when it comes to achieving something nearly impossible and the situation is absolutely difficult; the song "Strangers in the Night"[9], by the classic Metal group Saxon, where the powerful song vibrates as real as if we were passengers on the Boeing 747 mentioned in the lyrics:

> There's a 747 goin' into the night
> There's no power they don't know why
> They've no fuel they gotta land soon
> They can't land by the light of the moon
> They're overshooting there's no guiding lights

Noah had to option to deny God's request and find something better to do. Picture yourself in this situation, trying to find an almost impossible solution, like if on a high-speed plane, lost in the night trying to find in the dark a safe place to land. With the power down and without the system of guiding and orientation working, where the most optimistic perspective is the eminent disaster. In this situation, what could be done to avoid the worst?

The shorter answer would be to pray, trying to convince God and His angels to deliver the people from that evil. Or wait for a passenger with extraordinary abilities, as in the Hollywood movies, who would solve the situation in an improvised and bold fashion. I must confess that when hard times come, and the defeat and failure seem unavoidable, I think about one of quotes I like the best and I try to interpret differently: There is a remedy to everything, including death.

People tend to say there is a remedy for everything except death. I claim that if Jesus resurrected Lazarus and himself, we can assume or at least suppose there is a cure for death, which is yet to be revealed. Only Jesus had the medical expertise to reinstate biological life to those who lost it. There may be many metaphorical explanations about the resurrection of Lazarus, and what it meant to justify or assert in the Bible's narrative, but when it comes to Jesus, there is no denial that if we read expressively the texts of the New Testament, he indeed resurrected from the dead, spiritually and biologically.

Regardless of Bible's narratives, but considering that the human mind and positive attitudes can be differential assets who allow us to overcome any adversity, we can assume that most of the problems faced nowadays have a solution. Be it definitive or partial, it would allow us to at least keep trying to find alternatives, even for a final solution that differs from defeat or death.

Regarding the secret for the resurrection of dead bodies and minds, it may seem foolish to search for it today, although many of the largest scientific investments granted by modern corporations seek to reestablish dead tissues to life, and to enable humankind to free itself from the unacceptable grasp of death by prolonging its lifespan using biological, mechanical or hybrid means. In the second hypothesis, the technique of resurrection would be considered obsolete, as the prepondering modern scientific search is no longer the return of the dead, as proposed Jesus, but for the possibility of humans to ascend into eternity without dying beforehand, as wanted Woody Allen.

Nowadays, there are hundreds of people working for this goal, and certainly they belief it to be possible and reasonable on the long term. Considering, many modern humans no longer wish to resurrect in Christ and inhabit by his side on the alleged biblical paradise, from where God banished us thousands of years ago. Doubtless, these people invest loads of money on this type of research, for they intend to hang around forever on earth, enjoying life how they want, without any concern about following the Commandments that would set boundaries to their choices and their conquests. In order to achieve it, they must heavily invest in enhancing technologies that could improve, recover or at least "update" the biological composition of our organism, reinforcing the creed of overcoming the limitations God gave us by creating a superior human condition, which leads us to believe that "every new invention just puts another mile between us and the Garden of Eden".[20]

The search for biological resurrection of immortality is the most elevated boundary of human knowledge we can possibly dream, and fits perfectly in the need humankind always had of trying to attain the impossible, or making it at least partially possible according to the possibilities of time and space. Many of the research conducted on this field reinforce my belief that there is a remedy for everything in life, including death, even though seems unattainable for most people in our time. For some, however, it seems the supreme goal, an ideal to pursuit, a form of intimidate fulfillment or simply the recognition of a unprecedented achievement in the history of humankind, independent of God's help or Jesus' teachings.

The quest to make possible out of something allegedly impossible began at the very moment God expelled man and his wife from paradise, when they became aware of their higher intellectual capacities, as well as of their capacity of organization to carry out the daily tasks essential to collective survival in the dangerous world they started to inhabit.

According to the biblical narrative, God tasked armed angels to guard the gates of Heaven, as to prevent that man and women in regret returned to the garden on their own. Adam and Eve's descendants, however, decided on their own to impose themselves as the dominant species in the world, sharpening their intellectual skills to achieve the necessary means for building a better world than the lost Eden. A better world than the one God took from them, thus being able to rival with God themselves about their fate and the destiny of every other living being on Earth.

Seeking to do the impossible, many men and women started to systematically question the existence of God or if they were really created by Him. If God did not created us, though, it is possible to assume accurately that nowadays the perception humankind have of God is leading us to try to produce humans who come closer to said perception. It would be the greatest comical venture in human history: Humankind invented some sort of god it wanted to be when it "grew up". In other words, the human race created God just to match Him sometime in history. And for some people, this time is coming.

This little picture about gods and men only reinforces the belief that the each generations' problem have effective solutions given time, and nothing is impossible. Besides, it further corroborates the modern vision of the faith humankind has in itself, stressing more and more, overcoming the faith we historically devoted to gods for a long time.

In modern times, the belief that our bodies' biological death can be bypassed without God's help, although desired by many, is only shared by a few people. Even fewer are those who could effectively pay for such service, should it be available for sale. Still, even if it never happens, this search for eternal life will lead humankind into better techniques of recovery of our own bodies, and will certainly allow people to live hundreds of years, which is as good as forever by our modern standards. To other mortals, though, the search for immortality shows only that the song's Boeing 747, overshooting without guiding lights, without fuel or direction is the world where modern society lives in, the most common shared perception, especially in the military and academic environments. It represents strikingly well the idea of fleeing away from the Eden, landing somewhere else where it is possible to overlook the exaggerated impositions of God to the humankind in order to deliver it from death and misery, with the premise of existing a remedy for everything, including death.

The synthesis of central humankind line of thought on the last centuries can be resumed in; studying, knowing, working, building tools and machinery that can increase the power humans wish to possess over their own destiny and the destiny of the world as a whole, and trying to find efficient solutions for turning the impossible into a viable possibility. Even if we have to travel aimlessly, meaninglessly, producing a desperate anxiety where everyone will start to believe it is the right path to follow, despite the possibility of a plane-crashing taking with it humankind and its dreams to where everything started: powder and mud.

While human godhood is yet to be stablished, we still people of flesh, bone and nearly impossible dreams, and we must persist on the idea that there is a solution to every problem in life. Making apologies or avoiding guilty in the process only contributes to creating problems instead of solutions, among which demotivation, insensibility, disregarding one's own existence. Against those who would rather give up, there are people who, against all of the odds, continuously try to overcome the limitations of our own existence in a lost world amidst a no man's universe.

The motivation to only do the possible does not find any longer a support among the modern corporations, or among the most creative professionals who actually believe in the possible solutions to the hard tasks imposed, requiring only dedication, setting goals, defining processes and means to sooner or later achieving it, as it is essential to want to go beyond.

In a world far apart from ours, Noah built a boat and saved the animals while many believed he was mad or drunk, as the bible states he had a taste for wine. Even if this history is not entirely true, it can show that well motivated people can perform their jobs, when believing in the planned result, even if it is hard to achieve. In that case, the wanted result was to save all of the animal's life on Earth using sticks, stones, pitch and motivation to do it before a merciless torrent of water carried by God's wrath upon his creating.

People Will Always be Assets

Chico Buarque is one of the greatest names in this country's musical history, and resumes perfectly a little of Brazilian history and its migrating population in a beautiful song, where he claims his father was *paulista*, his grandfather was *pernambucano*, his great-grandfather was *mineiro*, and his great-great-grandfather, *baiano*. [21] Bringing this song to our own Amazon background, singers and groups like Antonio Pereira, Raízes Caboclas or Ave de Rapina could sing it as "my father is from Amazonas, my grandfather is from Acre, my great-grandfather is Cearense and my great-great-grandfather is Pernambucano". Countless people from Brazilian Northeast came to colonize the Amazon, especially after the drought of 1877, it's possible to assume that about 300-500 thousand northeasterners migrated. They formed bonds with the regional *caboclos,* the descendants of the many indigenous people, mixing different traits and contributing the cultural formation of the man in the Amazon[22] representing our culture in the Amazonas state ever since the Indigenous people came into contact with the European colonizers.

The massive migratory process to the Amazon stressed specially between 1880 and 1910, and had an abrupt decline the bankruptcy of the rubber industry. This economic sector would only resume its actives during World War II, when another draft of people from the North-east once again were encouraged into migrating to the North in order to work for the American war effort, imposed to Brazil's president Getúlio Vargas. It was unavoidable ever since the American general Lehman Miller claimed that the military bases in Belém and Recife would be occupied "for better or worse".[23] Without the resources to prevent the worse, Getúlio's government decided to offer the better, clearing the occupation of the military bases and "lending" Amazon as collateral for the financial loans and the transfer of industrial technologies yet inexistent in Brazil. These loans would improve the infrastructure of the more important economic poles in the south of the country, especially the construction of the National Steelyard Company on Rio the Janeiro, enabling the production of one of the time's main inputs: steel.

> With WW2, Amazon was drafted into the Allied effort, as the Japanese took over the oriental rubber and the synthetics' factories could no longer support the United States' demand. As a result, the Washington Agreements changed the life on the region, however did not improve it.[24]

At the closure of the Second World War, Brazilian federal government had already invested most of the money it earned from the Americans into the improvement of Southeast's infrastructure. It forgot, or never really bothered in telling the thousands of northeasterners that the war was over, and that they could go back to their homeland, without any credit or any right to the dollar division.

According to the accounts of some writers who visited towns in the Northeast during the great migration to the Amazon, in every harbor and ship, the absence of public agencies and employees to grant support was a heartbreaking message: those migrants would probably never come back. Facing the governmental oblivion, thousands of northeasterners never had the chance to go back home, and so they stayed, married, had children and lived essentially from the products of hunting, fishing, and the collection of tropical products, as the human ancestors have done for ten thousand years.

Those men and women had to make a living in the rich, desert and broad Amazon valley, reshaping the region's culture into what is now "caboclo-northeasterner", mixed through the bodies, pains, joys and traditions of the indigenous amazon on one hand, and the white, western, culture of the Sertão on the other. It lingered harmoniously through decades, legating, among other things, the culture of the Boi-bumbá party, and introducing many "original" words and pronunciations, as *"arigó"*, *"vermeio"*, *"mió"* and *"adonde"* to the amazon lexicon. After the insertion of the national television broadcast, that well-stablished cultural heritage clumsily absorbed the southeasterner culture, becoming essentially "caboclo-carioca", or "amarióca", derogatory term some of the more intellectual people from Manaus city use to describe caboclos or northerners who nourish a excess of love for the culture, traditions, rituals, soccer and behavior of the Rio de Janeiro people, the *cariocas*. As a result, many people tend to copy a bizarre, crippling version of Rio de Janeiro's lifestyle and culture.

However, my heritage is still completely caboclo-northeasterner. A wonderful combination of western European culture with the traditional indigenous culture from the Amazon, just as my parents received this culture from their parents, children of the countless miserable northeasterners who came to work in the Amazonas during that dark times, living in one of the thousands of rubber plantations along the sad and distant Purus river.

My grandfather was the son of a man born in Ceará, and he worked alongside his father in the rubber plantations. Probably he was illiterate and was certainly very catholic. I assume he was introspective, but everyone agreed he was a hard worker, he was deeply honest and strict with his children moral education. He told me few stories about his life, which should have been full of adventures and excitements, considering that life deep into the Amazon forest is still tough even nowadays, who would say in the decade of 1950, when the only source of information was a governmental radio station and the few boats who came by... Vaccines and schools were rare, and the services of government support were yet to exist. Besides, the great source of truths was the Bible, and the interpretations of the priests.

In one of the few conversations we had, he told me about a food shortage period, who fell upon the place he lived with his family, between 1950 and 1960. According to my grandfather, he tried to fish for several days and yet he found nothing to ease the hunger his family was going through, in a region where there were not many food markets to go shopping. Nor money enough to do so.

In one of these days of unproductive fishing, to make it even worse, the baits he took with him were over and he did not fish anything. In this tragic situation, a profound desperation took upon him and pain for he knew there was nothing back home to eat, and he could not expect anybody's aid in such an empty world. On the prime of his productive life and his mental faculties, having a wife and children to feed, he could not go back home and sadly say he could not offer nothing to offer as food.

Cornered between hunger, love for his children and lack of resources to perform an efficient job, my grandpa had the only option to chop of a chunk of his foot's sole and use it as bait, tucking it to the hook in hope of producing some effect that could bypass that desperate situation.

He threw the hook with a piece of his own flesh, and waited. For his surprise and luck, he caught a reasonable sized fish that could mitigate his family's hunger for a couple of days, besides, it could provide some time for his foot to heal. He forgot the pain and misery and rowed back home, to proudly inform his children that they would not starve.

To many people, this bold anecdote my grandpa used to tell me could be considered a sign of God, who came on his aid in the hard times. For others, it could have been an act of sheer luck, or even an exaggerated tale. To me, though, it presents an undeniable reality: sometimes, prayer, technologies and modern tools can fail to function as expected, or even the favorable conditions could suddenly change, and everything may seem to follow the path of defeat. Whenever it occurs, in an environment where apologies and failure are unacceptable, when the process cannot stop to correct itself, it is the bold action, aligned with human intelligence, that can overcome the difficulties imposed and take over the necessary risks in the search for unconventional but successful solutions, granting the safety of the process.

In any situation, out of necessity or imposition, the workers have to be proactive to be productive. They should always seek to work in a manner to predictably achieve their goals, efficiently, even if the external environment or the occasion do not offer the more favorable conditions. Even so, because the external conditions are always changing and the tools we have available are not always adapted to the new conditions, as in an economy whose only certainty is the uncertainty, the right source of everlasting competitive advantage is knowledge[25].

Tools, as computers, guns or the pitchfork work efficiently to those who skillfully study and comprehend its details, as any tool, even the most common and modern, can create more stress than showing solutions if the user does not possess basic acquaintance with its utilization. Besides, they can be wonderful auxiliaries when inserted or adapted into the process of efficient expertise.

In every culture, in any given time, it is possible to hear fantastical tales about people who managed to make a difference, without the necessary means to do it. Kings and heroes who thrived under the oddest situations, under the most contrary conditions. Legend or not, these narratives reinforce the human conviction that problems can be surpassed hen using as the main tool one's expertise or intelligence, when every other tools fail or are unavailable.

Moreover, many goals are not accomplished, many processes are interrupted and many projects fail daily, precisely because some people can only go as far as the conventional means end, not going further of what is clearly expressed in the textbooks and instructions. Only individuals can create knowledge, and life is a continuous interrelationship, dependent on people and processes tied to them. The solution to the daily problems on itself and to the problems who appears despite human interference can only be solved through the availability of people to solve it, on a pacific, inclusive, well-mannered interaction. Certainly, in given situations, people will the most important assets we can count on.

Even in the modern world, where a highly technological array of tools and gadgets can enhance the individual performance, quite often it is only the people's will and their disposition to face risks that can show the necessary solutions. Sometimes, solutions appear as urgent and unpostponable necessities to avoid a greater tragedy, as the situation of my grandpa, who had to be creative when the conventional solutions failed him. He needed to create a new work environment, when the traditional environment failed to meet his necessities.

Textbooks, manuals, work guidelines, anything dedicated to orient professionals about their performances and in a certain degree serve as some sort of evaluation, propose that conscious interaction between skills, attitudes and knowledge determine the path to practical expertise. They consider, yet, that knowledge without attitude, or skills without knowledge, limit the workers capacity to achieve complete results. But certainly those who can develop multiple skills to face a barrage of difficulties that comes when the conditions change and the options decrease, certainly do not feel any difference when lacking a tool or a conventional mean.

The greatest differential an enterprise can value, naturally, is the level of proactivity their professionals develop. In a certain way, it directly relates to their practical skills, also known as empirical knowledge. On my grandpa's case, his empirical knowledge was highly honed, especially because he knew he could not depend on anybody on the moments of extreme necessity besides his faith in God and the relatives who lived nearby, but struggled with the same conditions.

My grandpa disregarded any possibility of failure, and not accepting defeat as a final solution, he decided to try differently, adjusting the few tools he had available to the skills necessary to achieve the maximum result, which was fishing to eat. As a reward for his effort, he achieved it.

This is certainly only one of many situations he faced to survive in that forgotten world. If not for his extra skills, those not taught in graduate courses, his and my father's history could be deeply different, or even nonexistent, because hard and disciplined work, as life itself, requires a level of continuous effort much heavier than taught in books and guidelines. In abnormal situations, bot life and work require both a superior action skill, and besides disciplined knowledge, is the only form of building procedures and attitudes that will assure success and personal, familiar, or group survival.

What my grandpa taught me with this amazing story makes me remember of the beautiful song by the German Power Metal group Helloween, called "We Got the Right"[26] on the voice of the amazing lead singer Michael Kiske: Don't turn your head. Back to the wall. Don't close your eyes, And wait for your fall.

At last, Peace

Life is certainly much more than we expect it to be. It is the more dazzling adventure on the universe, and we will never get over or understand it completely, especially after losing it. As such, we should live and make an effort so that we and everyone else live, and live well. Learning, teaching and sharing with those who depends on us, at home, in the community, in the office, in empty and dark squares of overpopulated cities, humbly and conscious that we own no one but ourselves. That we are only the extension of our parents and grandparents lives, and we should pass it on with strength and clarity.

Modern medicinal practices and the better understanding of diseases' causes can prolong our physical and mental life and enable us to stay longer by the side of those we love. Even so, it also enabled the practice of work for a longer time span. If before we only had to learn until a certain age or practice, which slowly changed as the years went by, nowadays we have to learn how to learn at a much faster pace, as technologies, processes and operational routines change constantly.

As everything shall pass and end, do does our professional career too. Jobs pass by, processes change and companies hire and fire continuously. The world changes, while friends and networking remain alive for a little longer, as does the possibility of consolation if any difficulty shows up. We must be strong and firm, for when we reach the end of our professional career, we can look back proudly and look up hopefully, wanting to produce more but in a different environment, where the relationships are affective and collaborative, instead of business.

Considering that the world we were born into remained on the past a long time ago and we can no longer achieve it, we should face the new conditions life imposes as impossible to bypass. We should make our best to our children to comprehend that they are us, but in another conscience they build along their years of learning.

The greatest problem in human existence probably is our conscience that, among many things, developed a complex structure we call memory. This memory constitutes in a large catalogue of the precious souvenirs we preserved, just as the experiences and the remembrances of whom we loved and what we want for the future, what we tried to create. It makes us feel such a deep passion for ourselves through good memories we preserved that we refuse the idea of peacefully ceasing to exist someday, especially regarding the loss of our consciousness, the very reason for our existence. We will never accept the unavoidable fact of the physical death, and if not for the registers, memories, retirement and conscience of others, death would not have any psychological effect upon us. There would be not enough records to be lost forever, or to be selected into an alleged postmortem whose only importance would be to grand spiritual or mental life.

However, this is not an excuse to drop everything and wander desperately around the world, as Gilgamesh, searching for the body's immortality or the fountain of prolonged youth: many scientists, healers and modern wizards are dealing with the issue nowadays. On the contrary, we should seek to be happier and the more productive possible, while we have enough energy to endure any difficulty, while we can still keep trying and while the others and we still believe that we can overcome daily troubles. It was the mentality of the greatest warriors of the Antiquity, who would rather die chasing their life goals, which was basically winning battles, kidnapping or conquering women, leaving an heir and wait dying sickly for the end, in a anguishing elderly age, dull and without any merits for never trying to go further.

What death could be more fulfilling than the unexpected, defending the blood of our children and the honor of our ancestors, once said a great Roman politician.

Unfortunately, we cannot properly assert what happens after life is over, that is why the unexpected is thrilling and complex. We can only assume there is two distinct ways: One explained by the powerful song "Quest of Tanelorn", by the group Blind Guardian, where we will meet the *spiritus sanctus* and ascend into *vita aeterna*. Or the one as stated on the beautiful song "Hallowed be Thy Name", by Iron Maiden, that considers life down here is just a strange illusion… and nothing else.

Referências Capítulo V

1. Jean-Paul Sartre, **The Being and the Nothingness**
2. Bible
3. Anthony Giddens, **Consequences of Modernity**
4. Flávio Gikovake, **Mudar, Caminhos para a transformação verdadeira** 2014, p. 19
5. Iron Maiden, "**Hallowed be thy name**", in album "The Number of the Beast", 1981
6. Flávio Gikovake, **Mudar, Caminhos para a transformação verdadeira**, 2014, p. 85
7. Ikujiro Nonaka e Hirotaka Takeuchi, **On Knowledge Management**.
8. Directed by Andrew Niccol, 1997, Columbia Pictures.
9. Bob Dylan, "**The times they are a-changin'**", 1964, Columbia Records,
10. Directed by Frank Darabont, 1994, Columbia Pictures
11. Michel Foucault, **Microphysics of Power**.
12. Friedrich Engels, **Origin of the Family, Private Property, and the State,** 1884, p. 33
13. Bauman, **Liquid Modernity.**
14. Alan Greesnpan, **The Age of Turbulence**, 2007, p 397.
15. Jean Baudrillard, **Simulacra and Simulation**, 1981
16. Ikujiro Nonaka e Hirotaka Takeuchi, **On Knowledge Management**, p. 56
17. Mario Sergio Cortela, **não nascemos prontos**, p. 24
18. Alvin Tofler, **The Third Wave**
19. Saxon, "strangers in the night", album **Wheels of Steel**, 1980
20. Yuval Noah Harari, **Sapiens – A Brief History of Humankind**, p. 196
21. Chico Buarque, album **Para todos**
22. Djalma Batista, **O complexo da Amazônia**, 2ª edition, p.60.
23. Elio Gaspari, **A ditadura envergonhada**, As ilusões armadas,2014.
24. Djalma Batista, **O complexo da Amazônia**, 2ª edition, p.35
25. Ikujiro Nonaka e Hirotaka Takeuchi, **On Knowledge Management**.
26. Hellowen, Album **Keeper Of The Seven Kays**

> Um dia eu quero estar presente para ouvir meu povo cantar, como se fossem pássaros descendo sobre o ingazal. Descer o rio a vida inteira e com ele chegar ao mar, e em cada cachoeira que passar um copo pra me afogar.
> Antonio Pereira

VI – We in the Amazon

In the words of Anthony Giddens, *"the appropriation of knowledge does not happen in a homogeneous fashion, but is often differentially available to those in power positions"*[1]. However, despite the position someone hold in society, knowledge became essentially the differential tool of those who can use it properly, consciously adapting it to the countless process of interaction between man (or men) and environment.

The Amazon provides a huge source of natural resources, whose potential has yet to become appropriable knowledge to the benefit of its inhabitants, and considering that any simple possession of such resources does not assure any commercial or economical advantage to the region, the lack of a solid basis of knowledge generation nullifies every natural advantage. As a result, the Amazon drains itself waiting for any kind of intervention that could become an opportunity to the people scattered over its dense forest.

To Work for the Forest in a Jobless World?

In the Brazilian movie "Os Trapalhões e a Guerra dos Planetas", a space traveler while leaving his vessel, perceives the perplexity of the humans with his unexpected visitation, and says to them: "Do not worry, I came to ask for help. My planet is facing a crisis". Suddenly, the fool named Zacarias answer "So it's a tie, ours is too". In this aspect, in a not so far future, two questions will be more likely to instigate crisis and disorder in our country: how to find a job in a world with less and less formal employment, and how to feel comfortable and safe in an unstable job's market, where advanced systems of artificial intelligence may become the main administrative means of worldwide corporations?

Accordingly to data collected by the UN, offices and administrative sectors will be the more largely devastated in decreases of job offering, while the functions of administrative management – to manage software and systems – and financial management will request more capacitated professionals, who have more affinity with computational systems and are able to understand advanced mathematical schematizations, even beyond professionals of I.T. and Math. In other words, the world of future employment is the world of modern Scribes, specialized in the symbolic mathematical language bound to the construction of new systems of data collection, stocking and processing of the new economy.

On the other hand, an expressive part of scholars agree that most of the jobs who will be requested in the future are yet to be created, making impossible today for us to dream or determine the future careers we would like our children to follow. It leads us to the following question: what can be done to build, after the forest potential, to build a job-generating structure focused on attending the local population in a dignified, harmonious way? How can we create the professions we want our children to follow, before unemployment levels become even more critical?

If we do not have this answers, other possible option is to blackmail the rest of the world using the forest as a hostage – *laughter*.

In the deep countryside of the Amazon, the main sources of income are still the salaries paid to the public agents, retirement pensions and the local retailer commerce paid with the former salaries. Still today, a large amount of the population still living in a non-currency form of income, where the products extracted from the forest and the river plays an important role in assuring the maintenance of essential needs like food, habitation and transportation.

Since the decade of 1950, a large amount of Amazon's countryside migrated to the city of Manaus, hoping to find better conditions of life, study and work. The phenomenon intensified in the decades of 1980 and 1990, thanks to the possibility of finding work on Manaus' Free Economic Zone (FEZ) as a reaction to the near bankruptcy of the countryside economy, leading to the abandon of its population. In those decades, the economic activity in Manaus' Industrial Park needed essentially "intense" labor, since most of the companies did not have access to a stock of modern capital goods that could replace people and its workforce.

The economic opening, the globalization, the progressive insertion of automated systems and logistical equipment in the process of industrial production made possible the increasing growth in revenue of the Industrial Park without necessarily creating an expressive number of work posts, as the introduction of new technologies started to demand even fewer hires of laborers. In 2007, the revenue of the FEZ was nearly R$ 56 billion, with a total labor force of 89 thousand direct employees. In 2012, the revenue jumped to R$ 73 billion, generation 112 thousand direct jobs. In 2015, the Industrial Park revenue as only R$ 79 billion, with the average employment rate of 85 thousand jobs. In the stark comparison between 2007 and 2015, not considering the effects of the deep economic crisis that fell over the country, there was a reduction of 5% in the rate of direct employment, while the revenue of the companies (that did not broke) went up to a 30% raise. That explains why in 2017 the projects analyzed by the Council of Development in the State of Amazonas (CODAM, in the portuguese acronym) until the date of approval of the 257th amendment, approved the investment of around R$ 3 billion, generating only 1 thousand work posts. It means the new investments of the industries establishing its facilities in Manaus depends less and less on a huge workforce, needing only feel employees with an adequate level of knowledge. Beyond that, it is unlikely the dynamics of these new structures will be linked with the productive structures of the state's countryside, who is still regarded as a marginal, undesired partner to the great business that Manaus' FEZ represents to the country.

In this aspect, the importance of an efficient educational process, which produces enough levels of knowledge to assure the effective appropriation of the forest's resources become even more essential, considering that most of the better jobs in Amazonas's industries are filled by professionals issued from other states, and the *inequality in the labor field, be it on acquiring a job or its income, is related to the productive capacities, naturally involving knowledge.* [11]

Yet, we must consider the relative shortage of formal jobs in our state's industry, which should transfer this workforce to other "made-up" sectors or activities as a mean to keep any level of income, consumption and investment at an acceptable rate. Something must be done to keep the stat from falling again on complete bankruptcy of its more relevant activities, like happened to the Rubber industry in the 1910, or even worse: the workforce start to work for the ever-growing economical sector in the Amazon: the drug dealing.

If this scenario of progressive decline in corporate jobs is confirmed, what would be the relevant alternative to keeping the adequate economic levels, especially regarding employment and income?

How can we pave the way to this end, without devastating the forest's resources?

In the next decades, many jobs will be created, just as thousands of others will disappear, or will merge with others, or may acquire a new form. Currently, in a so-claimed post-industrial society, the Service Sector have been responsible for absorbing thousands of workers issued from Industrial Sector, "dismissed" thanks to the progressive lack of need of labor force in favor of automated, engineered process or the transfer of industrial facilities to new peripheral countries. Nevertheless, this process of absorption will not be infinite, most likely. The Service Sector is going through structural changes, for instance like happened to the bank services in the decade of 1980, which counted around 1 million workers, reducing this number by half on the decade of 1990. As such, we must assume the Services Sector will not be able to maintain a level of employment and high incomes, in similar conditions to the Industry in the 20th century.

Another hugely concerning question to the regional market's job is the temporal deadline to the fiscal incentives on Manaus' FEZ, as the optics of the system of tax renounces does not allow this type of incentive to go ad infinitum nor without any sort of compensation. The Constitutional Amendment 83/2014 postponed the incentives until the far away year of 2073, ending in a very different world from ours. However, the economic, environmental and social model we want to produce until there must be elaborated now, in this generation, so we can achieve a peaceful coordinated model of sustainable economic growth when the industrial model that allowed the insertion of the state of Amazonas in the global economy declines. This end should coincide with the end of the fossil fuel, allowing the introduction of new technologies, more advanced and clean, in the global systems around the world, where the Amazon will have an even more important role to the humanity on the post-oil and post-gas era.

Under this aspect, the governments and society main roles will be to invest on the scientific qualification of the citizens in the amazon, as to make possible the construction of a dynamic, efficient educational system, able to produce knowledge, brands and revenue to the region, especially on services that can only be delivered by deeply understanding the forest's biology and integrated systems. So, we must give meaning to the following questions:

- Why invest in ourselves?
- How to share knowledge about Amazon in a fair, safe way? How to internationalize Amazon without losing it?
- How to live in and for Amazon?

The Amazon is our greatest heritage and constitutes in the assurance we want to leave to our children and grandchildren.

Amazon and the Chemical Knowledge Society

In the last years, based on the knowledge about how our brain works under certain circumstances, many researches intended to analyze the functioning and the main brain links occurring in moments related to pleasure, sex, and happiness and other circumstantial manifestations of the individuals. Among the various researches, the ones who presented the more accurate conclusions were the ones who defined happiness, like other emotions, to an essentially chemical reaction, occurring when specific hormones are released in an individual's bloodstream, allowing him to feel happiness, sadness, pain or relief. Among these hormones, endorphin, serotonin and oxytocin are the ones directly related to the process of feeling happy. This discovery bears a huge weight in our society, where happiness is traditionally bound to a specific situation related to thought or existence, especially regarding professional, familiar and civic achievements, instead of a set of chemical reactions produced the individual's own body.

This fact also tries to explain why some people are absolutely miserable, and even though having access to the best resources, better company, better living conditions and specific pleasures cannot recognize themselves as happy. It is impossible to make those persons change their minds, because it is not their fault or someone's fault, only a biological ailment where the needed hormones needed to make them feel good are just not there, period. Thus, happiness is nothing but the result of chemicals produced in our organism randomly, never even considering that the humans consciously need to think themselves happy. Nonetheless, if, as some may say, to be successful is to be happy, then our body can easily receive the necessary amount of drugs to induce it to achieve success.

In this world, where knowledge is "absolute" and lots of the pleasures human beings crave are conceived in chemical terms, high-level scientists started to direct their researches to the development of chemical solutions who can induce the brain to release the feelings of pleasure, happiness and excitement. It could allow an individual to have full control of its emotions and unrestricted happiness in exchange of payment and ignorance that pure and plain chemical induction to pleasure may represent an even bigger threat than unhappiness. Beyond that, it overlooks that when miserable, people can at least listen to the sad songs of The Cure, Joy Division or Nick Cave without regrets, even showing happiness in misery.

The process of development the substances that causes reactions to the human organism, perceived as necessary to supply an existential need, has lead the pharmaceutical industry to develop countless substances that could induce unbound pleasure and limitless happiness, including the narcotics the international community condemn as illegal. The drug's market, especially synthetics, has grown beyond absurd everywhere in the world, especially in the central countries where a wide variety of drugs is produced, intended to serve the individual taste of its thousands of users, looking for chemically induced pleasures.

The industry of synthetic drugs has earned huge revenues and is on plain expansion, as would say the group Os Platinados, "who has mouth goes to Rome, but who has money goes to the mouth"[12]. People of all social backgrounds are invariably buying drugs they consider would make them feel good, searching for pleasure and freedom. This situation has generated an intense argument between those who defend the recreational use of drugs as a mean of pleasure, and those who disagree, *reason why the countries are fighting on an obstinate, bloody war against biochemical crimes*[13]. Among the drugs that claims to achieve "happiness" and "freedom" there are legal and illegal ones, being on the latter the business focus of criminal organizations, selling the concept of power and potency to the ones who consumes their products.

This bloody war is draws closer to our homes every day, flooding the news and expanding beyond our comprehension, leaving to the good citizens only the capacity to watch, in silence and patience, the daily scenes of daily horror in war more and more brutal. Because, in its core, it is not a war against organized crime and its violent systems, but a war against a culture who tries to impose itself as mainstream, defending happiness, pleasure, physical peak and extreme emotions as undeniable rights. Even though it means to achieve it by drugs highly destructive to the organism, produced upon an advanced basis of knowledge about the functioning of human brain and its substances.

  The greatest battle in the modern world is the fight against the growth of a cult following that defends openly the use of drugs as an important mean to achieve a specific end the organism itself cannot do. It is even legitimized by a structure of knowledge generation, being disciplined, monetized and globally connected, just like any structure in knowledge society.

  The criminal organizations focused on drugs production and distribution are only the material vessel of the substances those individuals want so badly to consume; be it for power, be it for leisure, be it for lack of control, be it for freedom or any other reason science and culture defines as important or essential. Because in the end, what matters truly is how much they will pay to get what they want or what they need, to assure the utilization of technology and advanced knowledge in the creation of new drugs.

  In this aspect, the Amazon region has been a reliable "partner" to the illegal drug industry, as the larger producers of cocaine in the world are found in its perimeter, using the rivers or the forest to hide, stock and ship a large part of their products through a structured network of "companies". In the process of reshaping the international drugs routes, beyond prioritizing the Amazon as main target of shipping, the drug lords managed to bring the production to places closer to the Brazilian Amazon.

  Brazil has been and still is absent in its operational responsibility for the production of knowledge that can assure safety, sustainability and appropriation of the forest's potential in favor of the amazon people, and, in case it did not notice the Amazon needs more investment that allows to know and to protect itself, and certainly a criminal organization will sooner or later, and without any remorse for the social and environmental damage it can cause.

This environment is deeply damaging to the a variety of sectors in our states' economy, especially to the companies who intend to create or expand business in the region, because beyond the economic difficulties and the horrifying logistic structure, they will still need to beware against the actions of criminals, that is as organized as a modern corporation, and in a way or another, uses the labor force that could be available to work in the Industrial Park or the FEZ.

Certainly, beyond many other problems that endure in the Amazon, the recent utilization of its structures by the illegal drug industry has become one of the toughest to deal with, because of its countless difficulties regarding insufficient data of the region. These problems reinforce the need of investment and the creation of an advanced system of knowledge that allows to know, to improve and to develop security policies needed for its own maintenance, by cleaner ends and favoring amazon's collectivity, without whom the regional future may never happen.

The Hub of Worldwide Knowledge

One of the hardest and more important tasks of any city in the modern world is to try to make it a safer, healthier, more pleasant and human place to the people and the companies who want to settle in to work, produce, live and share with society their results.

The modern world is a place of absolute competition, where people, companies and even cities and regions compete to attract productive incentives that can add in wealth, work, comfort and prosperity to its population, and allowing increases in tax revenue to the local governments. However, just as people prefer and crave to work in companies that can provide a higher level of security, comfort and professional growth, the companies too would rather settle in cities and regions where they would be assured safety, infrastructure, natural resources and specially a good basis of intellectual capital to assure the effectiveness of their business. The future's world is a world without actual jobs, whose main differential will be that the companies will demand intellectual capital. In this world, cities will compete among themselves to attract important companies that could guarantee their functioning as a political, social and economic entity, and the companies will most certainly prefer the cities who can offer the one resource they need the most: smart, creative, open and efficient people.

The cities who intend to compete for the attraction of those productive investments must start by largely invest themselves on the improvement of systems generating and passing knowledge as a way to assure some differential that may be relevant on the enterprises' decision about whether they should settle or not. An efficient system of educational is the greatest strategic resource to captivate the companies' eyes and investments.

In this aspect, the transformation of the industrial city, dirty and violated, to the knowledge city, technical, healthy and comfortable is a major challenge to the political and economic elites anywhere, and must become the focus of families, people and cities who want to get a better ranking in the world's social structures, quickly consolidating as post-industrial, post-modern and post-local.

Certainly, the construction of a society whose knowledge is the differential factor needs to follow up a reform in its obsolete structures that persists to endure on the inhabitants minds, like the absence of environmental responsibility, citizenship and respect for indigenous culture and traditions. It all comes down to the inexistence of a public structure of essential services that would help the citizens to feel safer and more comfortable and would help captivate investments and intellectual capital on the long-term. The raising of a modern, efficient pedagogic network is a necessary condition to change values and the build technologies that could make possible the operation of a shared system to assure the tranquility of the business and the integrity of the people who work on it, just like in the streets, in the schools, in the squares, homes and shared leisure places. The international organizations are multicultural, bringing to the cities they settle in a wide array of professionals of different nationalities and cultures who want to be well received, to interact in a respectful way the values and traditions of the locals who they will live and work with. As such, the natives and locals need to have conscience that the enterprises are structures of processing something useful to society, instead of an undeniable manifestation of an imperialistic purpose who they must ruthlessly combat.

Another fundamental point to the improvement of the living standards in most major cities – especially Manaus – but without any possible solution anytime soon is the urban traffic and public transportation structure. Its precariousness aggravates every generation and bears a huge weight on the companies' decision, because part of their revenues results in business around the globe, and they need an efficient structure to dispose their products at the lowest cost and quickest as possible. The cities who cannot neither receive nor dispose goods effectively is bound to score negative at the global investment map.

Still considering the modern world as the world of high-voltage information, like the first album of Australian group AC/DC, the modern cities need to have at their disposal a potent form of energy and high-speed means of communication, being the necessities of capital importance of the knowledge society, without whom it cannot even exist.

Looking at the wide Amazon region it is easy to perceive there is a large gap between what the companies need as minimum to persist here, and what our impoverished cities can provide, where only Manaus have the differential of the FEZ to of offer to its investors. Outside the fiscal incentives, the city has yet to manage a fundamental, wide and modern infrastructure to make possible for the companies to settle in indefinitely.

Most of the Amazon towns offer nothing but cheap labor force and vast reserves of natural resources as differential, like oil and natural gas in Coari and niobium in São Gabriel, a metal that while so needed to the cutting edge technology, still have not a single company who can process it in national territory.

As such, the cities in Amazon still follow their via-crucis, without conditions to offer the minimum of the structures the companies needs to settle in, and without the means to explore the immense resources of the forest due to the lack of knowledge needed to do it without harming the environment. The fundamental question remains; until when should we wait, without having to knee down and waiting for God's help to invert this precarious situation and without needing to cut down the forest?

The Microphysics of Knowing

To end this work, I have decided to make an analogy to the great work of Michael Foucault, aimed at studying the characteristics of the power relations, that determines other types of social relations manifesting themselves in a particular way on a daily basis. As he asserts, what makes possible for power structures to remain solid and efficient is that *power does not only weight as a force saying "no", but because it allows for the production of things, induces to pleasure, generates knowledge and produces a speech, and it reproduces relations from barely noticeable mechanisms, as the exercise of power creates a productive network that embraces all of the social body*[14.]

In every modern society, knowledge relies on many other aspects that goes beyond the simple considerations and determinations of the process of knowing and understanding, by re-writing traditions and imposing itself as the structuring force rationalizing the historical-social context, conditioning every aspect of life: from war to sex. One of the main questions in this work is to demonstrate how the modern value represented by knowledge is changing our lives, as much as its capacities and consequences. Through knowledge, we are changing our perception about gods and religions, our relation with ethical values, changing how we see ourselves and especially how the government and institutions perceive people and the economic process, producing a wide remodeling in relations with family, in living and working conditions and in the system of generating and excluding knowledge, and the necessity of a rediscovery of another meaning for personal and social life.

Wars, famine, disasters and natural catastrophes have widened even more the number of refugees in search of work, safety, protection and food in countries away from their horror and misery. The world always faced crisis and regional wars, which soon became global when the codependence of countries became more widespread and failed to mitigate the over appropriation of world's richness. Nonetheless, the causes for these events are being redefined by the new traits of modern thinking, where material things are more valued than humans' lives and local traditions are being torn apart by the globalized world trying to include all of humankind in the same process of evolution, development, and defined values that should be shared as the only ones.

Humankind is everyday further apart from itself, walking into the path of dynamism and reliance on technological intervention in every aspect of life. If on the beginning of human trajectory, knowledge meant to understand God and His intentions, the goals now are to create tools that makes us independent from God. In this new world, the extra-human dependence is for more technologies, who could allow us to live longer, better, more comfortable and for some, free of any moral boundaries, as a cureless cancer or a vicious drug.

Referência Capítulo VI

1. Anthony Giddens, **The Consequences of Modernity**, p. 44
2. Samuel Benchimol, **Amazonia Formação Social e Cultural**, p. 479
3. Ibdem, p. 480.
4. IBGE
5. Marcio Souza, **A expressão amazonense**
6. Djalma Batista, **o complexo da Amazônia**, p. 379.
7. IBGE Bureau of national accounts, 1999
8. Yuval Noah Harari, **Sapiens – a Brief History of Humanankind**.
9. Samuel Benchimol, **Amazônia Formação Social e Cultural**, p. 508
10. SUFRAMA/COISE/CGPRO/SAPhttp://site.suframa.gov.br/noticias/pim-fatura
11. José Lopes da Silva, **Amazonas, do extrativismo à industrialização** p. 704
12. Lyrics to the song "**Trajetória**", by Manaus' based rock band Platinados. In Brazilian Portuguese, it plays with a common saying that says "Who has a mouth, goes to Rome", meaning that those who can express themselves can go anywhere. Also, "mouth" in Brazil is a slang for the place where drugs are bought.
13. Yuval Noah Harari, **Homo Deus**.
14. Michael Foulcaut, **Microphysics of Power**

www.ingramcontent.com/pod-product-compliance
Lightning Source LLC
Chambersburg PA
CBHW030632220526
45463CB00004B/1496